THE BI
EMBARRASSING MOMENTS

Contains Portions of the Old and New Testaments

Compiled from the King James Translation with
all Standard Bibles Diligently Compared and Revised

––––––––––––––––––––

"Search the scriptures: for in them ye think ye have eternal
life." — John v, 39.

"All scripture is given by inspiration of God, and is
profitable for   doctrine, for reproof, for correction, for
instruction in righteousness."

— 2 Tim. iii, 16.

––––––––––––––––––––

FIRST PUBLISHED IN NEW YORK BY:
INDEPENDENT BIBLE SOCIETY,
INSTITUTED IN THE YEAR MDCCCLXVII.

REPRINTED 1999
The Book Tree
Escondido, California

The Bible's Most Embarrassing Moments
ISBN 1-58509-025-5

©1999
The Book Tree
All Rights Reserved

Republished 1999 by
The Book Tree
Post Office Box 724
Escondido, CA 92033

Call (800) 700-TREE for a FREE BOOK TREE CATALOG
with over 1000 Books, Booklets, Audio, and Video on
Alchemy, Ancient Mysteries, Anti-Gravity, Atlantis, Free
Energy, Gnosticism, Health Issues, Magic, Metaphysics,
Mythology, Occult, Rare Books, Religious Controversy,
Sitchin Studies, Spirituality, Symbolism, Tesla, and much
more. Or visit our website at www.thebooktree.com

INDEX.

INDEX.

INDEX.

INDEX

INDEX.

BIBLE'S MOST EMBARRASSING MOMENTS

INTRODUCTION

I was totally amazed with this book because it is nothing more than the Bible. Choice parts of the Bible, but the Bible nonetheless.

The cast of characters in this book is incredible, and you never know what will happen next. They should consider making this part of the "good book" into a movie, since Hollywood thrives on things like sex and treachery. It is filled with thieves, liars, whores and killers, to name a few, including the major star and king of all culprits, Jehovah.

Jehovah takes the cake when it comes to killing innocent people (including babies) and making up nit-picking rules. He plays a big role in many terrible events found in these pages, while the people themselves, without God's influence, engage in as much hanky-panky as you could find on the afternoon soap operas.

If the Bible is supposed to be a guidebook for moral conduct, these are the parts they should edit out. Who knows — some of the worst scoundrels in history might have used these passages as an excuse for terrible deeds. "If God butchered all kinds of innocent people then why the hell can't I do it, in His name?" That seems to be a pattern in history.

I am a minister of the Gnostic tradition. The Gnostics were considered heretics by the early Christian fathers because they believed that instead of going into a church and being told what to believe, you could experience God for yourself. Religion was being "organized" by the church so you couldn't have people doing their own thing. It caused too much trouble and confusion for those in power, and gave them less control over the masses. Instead of experiencing God, they wanted you to simply accept Him. To have faith instead of knowledge. Think about it. Would you rather just trust in God, or do you want to experience Him?

If you want true knowledge, you do not accept blindly. You must ask questions. Do not accept what "they" tell you. Question them. Work in your own special way to discover meaning and purpose in your life. Don't let your meaning and purpose be dictated to you.

That is what makes these Bible selections so interesting. They cause you to think, and to question. Although they will shock you, and titillate you, examine them carefully and give them some thought. I am not trying to convince you to reject the entire Bible. Many things in it are useful, but again, much should be questioned.

There is a difference between being religious and being spiritual. You are first and foremost a spiritual being. Religion is for the masses, spirituality is for the individual. Read this, grow and be yourself.

Paul Tice

GENESIS.

Chap. II.

21 And the Lord God caused a deep sleep to fall upon Adam, and he slept; and he took one of his ribs, and closed up the flesh instead thereof.

22 And the rib, which the Lord God had taken from man, made he a woman, and brought her unto the man.

23 And Adam said, This *is* now bone of my bones, and flesh of my flesh: she shall be called Woman, because she was taken out of man.

25 And they were both naked, the man and his wife, and were not ashamed.

Chap. III.

7 And the eyes of them both were opened, and they knew that they *were* naked: and they sewed fig-leaves together, and made themselves aprons.

9 And the Lord God called unto Adam, and said unto him, Where *art* thou?

10 And he said, I heard thy voice in the garden: and I was afraid, because I *was* naked; and I hid myself.

11 And he said, Who told thee that thou *wast* naked?

16 Unto the woman he said, I will greatly multiply thy sorrow and thy conception; in sorrow thou shalt bring forth children: and thy desire *shall be* to thy husband, and he shall rule over thee.

Chap. IV.

1 And Adam knew Eve his wife; and she con-ceived, and bare Cain, and said, I have gotten a man from the LORD.

2 And she again bare his brother Abel.

25 And Adam knew his wife again, and she bare a son, and called his name Seth.

Chap. VI.

1 And it came to pass, when men began to mul-tiply on the face of the earth, and daughters were born unto them,

2 That the sons of God saw the daughters of men that they *were* fair; and they took them wives of all which they chose.

4 The sons of God came in unto the daughters of men, and they bare *children* to them.

Chap. IX.

20 And Noah began *to be* an husbandman, and he planted a vineyard:

21 And he drank of the wine, and was drunken; and he was uncovered within his tent.

22 And Ham, the father of Canaan, saw the nakedness of his father, and told his two brethren without.

23 And Shem and Japheth took a garment, and laid *it* upon both their shoulders, and went back-ward, and covered the nakedness of their father: and their faces *were* backward, and they saw not their father's nakedness.

24 And Noah awoke from his wine, and knew what his younger son had done unto him.

25 And he said, Cursed *be* Canaan; a servant of servants shall he be unto his brethren.

26 And he said, Blessed *be* the LORD God of Shem; and Canaan shall be his servant.

Chap. XI.

30 But Sarai was barren; she *had* no child.

Chap. XII.

10 And there was a famine in the land: and Abraham went down into Egypt to sojourn there; for the famine *was* grievous in the land.

11 And it came to pass, when he was come near to enter into Egypt, that he said unto Sarai his wife, Behold now, I know that thou *art* a fair woman to look upon:

12 Therefore it shall come to pass, when the Egyptians shall see thee, that they shall say, This *is* his wife: and they will kill me, but they will save thee alive.

13 Say, I pray thee, thou *art* my sister: that it may be well with me for thy sake; and my soul shall live because of thee.

14 And it came to pass, that when Abram was come into Egypt, the Egyptians beheld the woman that she *was* very fair.

15 The princes also of Pharaoh saw her, and commended her betore Pharaoh: and the woman was taken into Pharaoh's house.

16 And he entreated Abram well for her sake: and he had sheep, and oxen, and he-asses, and men-servants, and maid-servants, and she-asses, and camels.

17 And the Lord plagued Pharaoh and his house with great plagues because of Sarai, Abram's wife.

18 And Pharaoh called Abram, and said, What *is* this *that* thou hast done unto me? why didst thou not tell me that she *was* thy wife?

19 Why saidst thou, She *is* my sister? so I might have taken her to me to wife: now therefore behold thy wife, take *her*, and go thy way.

20 And Pharaoh commanded *his* men concerning him: and they sent him away, and his wife, and all that he had.

Chap. XVI.

1 Now Sarai, Abram's wife, bare him no children: and she had an handmaid, an Egyptian, whose name *was* Hagar.

2 And Sarai said unto Abram, Behold now, the Lord hath restrained me from bearing: I pray thee go in unto my maid; it may be that I may obtain children by her: and Abram hearkened to the voice of Sarai.

3 And Sarai, Abram's wife, took Hager her maid the Egyptian, after Abram had dwelt ten years in the land of Canaan, and gave her to her husband Abram to be his wife.

4 And he went in unto Hagar, and she conceived: and when she saw that she had conceived, her mistress was despised in her eyes.

5 And Sarai said unto Abram, My wrong *be* upon thee: I have given my maid into thy bosom; and when she saw that she had conceived, I was despised in her eyes: the Lord judge between me and thee.

6 But Abram said unto Sarai, Behold, thy maid *is* in thy hand; do to her as it pleaseth thee. And when Sarai dealt hardly with her, she fled from her face.

7 And the angel of the Lord found her by a fountain of water in the wilderness, by the fountain in the way to Shur.

8. And he said, Hagar, Sarai's maid, whence camest thou? and whither wilt thou go? And she said, I flee from the face of my mistress Sarai.

9 And the angel of the Lord said unto her,

Return to thy mistress, and submit thyself under her hands.

10 And the angel of the Lord said unto her, I will multiply thy seed exceedingly, that it shall not be numbered for multitudes.

11 And the angel of the Lord said unto her, Behold, thou *art* with child, and shalt bear a son: and shalt call his name Ishmael; because the Lord hath heard thy affliction.

15 And Hagar bare Abram a son, and Abram called his son's name, which Hagar bare, Ishmael.

CHAP. XVII.

1 And when Abram was ninety years old and nine, the Lord appeared to Abram, and said unto him, I *am* the Almighty God; walk before me, and be thou perfect.

2 And I will make my covenant between me and thee, and will multiply thee exceedingly.

6 And I will make thee exceeding fruitful, and I will make nations of thee; and kings shall come out of thee.

9 And God said unto Abraham, Thou shalt keep my covenant therefore, thou, and thy seed after thee, in their generations.

10 This *is* my covenant, which ye shall keep, between me and you, and thy seed after thee: Every man-child among you shall be circumcised.

11 And ye shall circumcise the flesh of your foreskin; and it shall be a token of the covenant betwixt me and you.

12 And he that is eight days old shall be circumcised among you, every man-child in your generations, he that is born in the house, or bought with money of any stranger which *is* not of thy seed.

13 He that is born in thy house, and he that is

bought with thy money, must needs be circumcised : and my covenant shall be in your flesh for an everlasting covenant.

14 And the uncircumcised man-child, whose flesh of his foreskin is not circumcised, that soul shall be cut off from his people; he hath broken my covenant.

15 And God said unto Abraham, As for Sarai thy wife, thou shalt not call her name Sarai, but Sarah *shall* her name *be.*

16 And I will bless her, and give thee a son also of her: yea, I will bless her, and she shall be *a mother* of nations; kings of people shall be of her.

17 Then Abraham fell upon his face, and laughed, and said in his heart, Shall *a child* be born unto him that is an hundred years old? and shalt Sarah, that is ninety years old, bear?

18 And Abraham said unto God, O that Ishmael might live before thee!

19 And God said, Sarah thy wife shall bear thee a son indeed; and thou shalt call his name Isaac: and I will establish my covenant with him for an everlasting covenant, *and* with his seed after him.

20 And as for Ishmael, I have heard thee : Behold, I have blessed him, and will make him fruitful, and will multiply him exceedingly : twelve princes shall he beget, and I will make him a great nation.

21 But my covenant will I establish with Isaac, which Sarah shall bear unto thee at this set time in the next year.

22 And he left off talking with him, and God went up from Abraham.

23 And Abraham took Ishmael his son, and all that were born in his house, and all that were

bought with his money, every male among the men of Abraham's house; and circumcised the flesh of their foreskin, in the self-same day, as God had said unto him.

24 And Abraham *was* ninety years old and nine, when he was circumcised in the flesh of his foreskin.

25. And Ishmael his son *was* thirteen years old, when he was circumcised in the flesh of his foreskin.

26 In the self-same day was Abraham circumcised, and Ishmael his son;

27 And all the men of his house, born in the house, and bought with money of the stranger, were circumcised with him.

Chap. XVIII.

1 And the Lord appeared unto him in the plains of Mamre: and he sat in the tent door in the heat of the day.

2 And he lifted up his eyes and looked, and, lo, three men stood by him.

9 And they said unto him, Where *is* Sarah thy wife? And he said, Behold, in the tent.

10 And he said, I will certainly return unto thee according to the time of life; and, lo, Sarah thy wife shall have a son. And Sarah heard *it* in the tent door, which *was* behind him.

11 Now Abraham and Sarah *were* old *and* well stricken in age; *and* it ceased to be with Sarah after the manner of women.

12 Therefore Sarah laughed within herself, saying, After I am waxed old shall I have pleasure, my lord being old also?

13 And the Lord said unto Abraham, Wherefore did Sarah laugh, saying, Shall I of a surety bear a child, which am old?

14 Is anything too hard for the LORD? At the time appointed I will return unto thee, according to the time of life, and Sarah shall have a son.

15 Then Sarah denied, saying, I laughed not; for she was afraid. And he said, Nay; but thou didst laugh.

16 And the men rose up from thence and looked toward Sodom.

CHAP. XIX.

1 And there came two angels to Sodom at even; and Lot sat in the gate of Sodom: and Lot seeing *them* rose up to meet them; and he bowed himself with his face toward the ground:

2 And he said, Behold now, my lords, turn in, I pray you, into your servant's house, and tarry all night, and wash your feet, and ye shall rise up early, and go on your ways. And they said, Nay; but we will abide in the street all night.

3 And he pressed upon them greatly; and they turned in unto him, and entered into his house; and he made them a feast, and did bake unleavened bread, and they did eat.

4 But before they lay down, the men of the city, *even* the men of Sodom, compassed the house round, both old and young, all the people from every quarter:

5 And they called unto Lot, and said unto him, Where *are* the men which came in to thee this night? bring them out unto us, that we may know them.

6 And Lot went out at the door unto them, and shut the door after him.

7 And said, I pray you, brethren, do not so wickedly.

8 Behold now, I have two daughters which have not known man; let me, I pray you, bring them out unto you, and do ye to them as *is* good in your

eyes: only unto these men do nothing; for therefore came they under the shadow of my roof.

9 And they said, Stand back. And they said *again*, This one *fellow* came in to sojourn, and he will needs be a judge: now will we deal worse with thee than with them. And they pressed sore upon the man, *even* Lot, and came near to break the door.

10 But the men put forth their hand, and pulled Lot into the house to them, and shut to the door.

11 And they smote the men that *were* at the door of the house with blindness, both small and great: so that they wearied themselves to find the door.

12 And the men said unto Lot, Hast thou here any besides? son-in-law, and thy sons, and thy daughters, and whatsoever thou hast in the city, bring *them* out of this place:

13 For we will destroy this place, because the cry of them is waxen great before the face of the LORD; and the LORD hath sent us to destroy it.

14 And Lot went out, and spake unto his sonsin-law, which married his daughters, and said, Up, get you out of this place; for the LORD will destroy this city: but he seemed as one that mocked unto his sons-in-law.

15 And when the morning arose, then the angels hastened Lot, saying, Arise, take thy wife, and thy two daughters which are here, lest thou be consumed in the iniquity of the city.

16 And while he lingered, the men laid hold upon his hand, and upon the hand of his wife, and upon the hand of his two daughters; the LORD being merciful unto him; and they brought him forth, and set him without the city.

22 Haste thee, escape thither; for I cannot do

anything till thou be come thither: therefore the name of the city was called Zoar.

23 The sun was risen upon the earth when Lot entered into Zoar.

24 Then the LORD rained upon Sodom and upon Gomorrah brimstone and fire from the LORD out of heaven;

25 And he overthrew those cities, and all the plain, and all the inhabitants of the cities, and that which grew upon the ground.

26 But his wife looked back from behind him, and she became a pillar of salt.

30 And Lot went up out of Zoar, and dwelt in the mountain, and his two daughters with him; for he feared to dwell in Zoar: and he dwelt in a cave, he, and his two daughters.

31 And the first-born said unto the younger, Our father *is* old, and *there is* not a man in the earth to come in unto us after the manner of all the earth:

32 Come, let us make our father drink wine, and we will lie with him, that we may preserve the seed of our father.

33 And they made their father drink wine that night: and the first-born went in, and lay with her father; and he perceived not when she lay down, nor when she arose.

34 And it came to pass on the morrow, that the first-born said unto the younger, Behold, I lay yesternight with my father: let us make him drink wine this night also; and go thou in, *and* lie with him, that we may preserve seed of our father.

35 And they made their father drink wine that night also: and the younger arose, and lay with him; and he perceived not when she lay down nor when she arose.

36 Tɪ as were both the daughters of Loʊ with child by their father.

37 And the first-born bare a son, and called his name Moab: the same *is* the father of the Moabites unto this day.

38 And the younger, she also bare a son, and called his name Ben-ammi: the same *is* the father of the children of Ammon unto this day.

Chap. XX.

1 And Abraham journeyed from thence toward the south country, and dwelt between Kadesh and Shur, and sojourned in Gerar.

2 And Abraham said of Sarah his wife, She *is* my sister: and Abimelech king of Gerar sent, and took Sarah.

3 But God came to Abimelech in a dream by night, and said to him, Behold, thou *art but* a dead man, for the woman which thou hast taken: for she *is* a man's wife.

4 But Abimelech had not come near her: and he said, LORD, wilt thou slay also a righteous nation?

5 Said he not unto me she is my sister? and she, even she herself said, He *is* my brother: in the integrity of my heart and innocency of my hands have I done this.

6 And God said unto him in a dream, Yea, I know that thou didst this in the integrity of thy heart: for I also withheld thee from sinning against me: therefore I suffered thee not to touch her.

7 Now therefore restore the man *his* wife: for he *is* a prophet, and he shall pray for thee, and thou shalt live: and if thou restore *her* not, know thou that thou shalt surely die, thou, and all that *are* thine.

8 Therefore Abimelech rose early in the morn·
ing, and called all his servants, and told all these
things in their ears : and the men were sore afraid.

9 Then Abimelech called Abraham, and said
unto him, What hast thou done unto us? and
what have I offended thee, that thou hast brought
on me and on my kingdom a great sin? thou hast
done deeds unto me that ought not to be done.

10 And Abimelech said unto Abraham, What
sawest thou, that thou hast done this thing?

11 And Abraham said, Because I thought,
Surely the fear of God *is* not in this place: and
they will slay me for my wife's sake.

12 And yet indeed *she is* my sister : she *is* the
daughter of my father, but not the daughter of my
mother; and she became my wife.

13 And it came to pass, when God caused me to
wander from my father's house, that I said unto
her, This *is* thy kindness which thou shalt shew
unto me: at every place whither we shall come
say of me, He *is* my brother.

14 And Abimelech took sheep, and oxen, and
men-servants, and woman-servants, and gave *them*
unto Abraham, and restored him Sarah his wife.

15 And Abimelech said, Behold, my land *is*
before thee ; dwell where it pleaseth thee.

16 And unto Sarah he said, Behold, I have given
thy brother a thousand *pieces* of silver : behold, he
is to thee a covering of the eyes, unto all that *are*
with thee, and with all *other :* thus she was re-
proved.

17 So Abraham prayed unto God : and God
healed Abimelech, and his wife, and his maid-servants; and they bare *children.*

18 For the LORD had fast closed up all the
wombs of the house of Abimelech, because of
Sarah, Abraham's wife.

Chap. XXI.

1 And the LORD visited Sarah as he had said, and the LORD did unto Sarah as he had spoken.

2 For Sarah conceived, and bare Abraham a son in his old age, at the set time of which God had spoken to him.

3 And Abraham called the name of his son that was born unto him, whom Sarah bare to him, Isaac.

4 And Abraham circumcised his son Isaac being eight days old, as God had commanded him.

5 And Abraham was a hundred years old, when his son Isaac was born unto him.

6 And Sarah said, God hath made me to laugh, *so that* all that hear will laugh with me.

7 And she said, Who would have said unto Abraham, that Sarah should have given children suck? for I have borne *him* a son in his old age.

8 And the child grew, and was weaned: and Abraham made a great feast the *same* day that Isaac was weaned.

Chap. XXII.

23 And Bethuel begat Rebekah : these eight Milcah did bear to Nahor, Abraham's brother.

24 And his concubine, whose name *was* Reumah, she bare also Tebah, and Gaham, and Thahash, and Maachah.

Chap. XXIV.

16 And the damsel *was* very fair to look upon, a virgin; neither had any man known her: and she went down to the well, and filled her pitcher, and came up.

Chap. XXV.

1 Then again Abraham took a wife, and her name *was* Keturah.

2 And she bare him Zimran, and Jokshan, and Medan, and Midian, and Ishbak, and Shuah.

6 But unto the sons of the concubines which A'raham had, Abraham gave gifts, and sent them away from Isaac his son.

21 And Isaac entreated the LORD for his wife, because she *was* barren: and the LORD was entreated of him, and Rebekah his wife conceived.

22 And the children struggled together within her: and she said, If *it be* so, why *am* I thus? And she went to inquire of the LORD.

23 And the LORD said unto her, Two nations *are* in thy womb, and two manner of people shall be separated from thy bowels: and *the one* people shall be stronger than *the other* people; and the elder shall serve the younger.

24 And when her days to be delivered were fulfilled, behold, *there were* twins in her womb.

25 And the first came out red, all over like an hairy garment: and they called his name Esau.

26 And after that came his brother out, and his hand took hold on Esau's heel; and his name was called Jacob: and Isaac *was* threescore years old when she bare them.

CHAP. XXVI.

6 And Isaac dwelt in Gerar:

7 And the men of the place asked *him* of his wife, and he said, She *is* my sister: for he feared to say, *She is* my wife; lest, *said he*, the men of the place should kill me for Rebekah; because she *was* fair to look upon.

8 And it came to pass when he had been there a long time, that Abimelech king of the Philistines looked out at a window, and saw, and behold, Isaac *was* sporting with Rebekah his wife.

9 And Abimelech called Isaac, and said, Be-

hold, of a surety she *is* thy wife: and how saidst thou, She *is* my sister? And Isaac said unto him, Because I said, Lest I die for her.

10 And Abimelech said, What *is* this thou hast done unto us? one of the people might lightly have lien with thy wife, and thou shouldst have brought guiltiness upon us.

11 And Abimelech charged all *his* people, saying, He that toucheth this man or his wife shall surely be put to death.

Chap. XXIX.

15 And Laban said unto Jacob, Because thou *art* my brother, shouldest thou therefore serve me for nought? tell me, what *shall* thy wages *be?*

16 And Laban had two daughters: the name of the elder *was* Leah, and the name of the younger *uas* Rachel.

17 Leah *was* tender-eyed, but Rachel was beautiful and well-favored.

18 And Jacob loved Rachel; and said, I will serve thee seven years for Rachel thy younger daughter.

19 And Laban said, *It is* better that I give her to thee, than that I should give her to another man: abide with me.

20 And Jacob served seven years for Rachel; and they seemed unto him *but* a few days, for the love he had to her.

21 And Jacob said unto Laban, Give *me* my wife (for my days are fulfilled) that I may go in unto her.

22 And Laban gathered together all the men of the place, and made a feast.

23 And it came to pass in the evening, that he took Leah his daughter, and brought her to him; and he went in unto her.

24 And Laban gave unto his daughter Leah, Zilpah his maid, *for* an handmaid.

25 And it came to pass, that in the morning, behold, it *was* Leah: and he said to Laban, What *is* this thou hast done unto me? did not I serve thee for Rachel? wherefore then hast thou beguiled me?

26 And Laban said, It must not be so done in our country, to give the younger before the firstborn.

27 Fulfil her week, and we will give thee this also, for the service which thou shalt serve with me yet seven other years.

28 And Jacob did so, and fulfilled her week: and he gave him Rachel his daughter to wife also.

29 And Laban gave to Rachel his daughter, Bilhah his handmaid, to be her maid.

30 And he went in also unto Rachel, and he loved also Rachel more than Leah, and served with him yet seven other years.

31 And when the LORD saw that Leah *was* hated, he opened her womb: but Rachel *was* barren.

32 And Leah conceived, and bare a son; and she called his name Reuben: for she said, Surely the LORD hath looked upon my affliction; now therefore my husband will love me.

33 And she conceived again, and bare a son; and said, Because the LORD hath heard that I *was* hated, he hath therefore given me this *son* also: and she called his name Simeon.

34 And she conceived again, and bare a son; and said, Now this time will my husband be joined unto me, because I have borne him three sons: therefore was his name called Levi.

35 And she conceived again, and bare a son: and she said, Now will I praise the LORD: therefore she called his name Judah; and left bearing.

Chap. XXX.

1 And when Rachel saw that she bare Jacob no children, Rachel envied her sister; and said unto Jacob, Give me children, or else I die.

2 And Jacob's anger was kindled against Rachel; and he said, *Am* I in God's stead, who hath withheld from thee the fruit of the womb?

3 And she said, Behold my maid Bilhah, go in unto her; and she shall bear upon my knees, that I may also have children by her.

4 And she gave him Bilhah her handmaid to wife: and Jacob went in unto her.

5 And Bilhah conceived, and bare Jacob a son.

6 And Rachel said, God hath judged me, and hath also heard my voice, and hath given me a son; therefore called she his name Dan.

7 And Bilhah, Rachel's maid, conceived again, and bare Jacob a second son.

8 And Rachel said, With great wrestlings have I wrestled with my sister, and I have prevailed; and she called his name Naphtali.

9 When Leah saw that she had left bearing, she took Zilpah, her maid, and gave her Jacob to wife.

10 And Zilpah, Leah's maid, bare Jacob a son.

11 And Leah said, A troop cometh: and she called his name Gad.

12 And Zilpah, Leah's maid, bare Jacob a second son.

13 And Leah said, Happy am I, for the daughters will call me blessed: and she called his name Asher.

14 And Reuben went in the days of wheat-harvest, and found mandrakes in the field, and brought them unto his mother Leah. Then Rachel said to Leah, Give me, I pray thee, of thy son's mandrakes,

15 And she said unto her, *Is it* a small **matter** that thou hast taken my husband? and wouldest thou take away my son's mandrakes also? And Rachel said, Therefore he shall lie with thee to-night for thy son's mandrakes.

16 And Jacob came out of the field in the evening, and Leah went out to meet him, and said, Thou must come in unto me; for surely I have hired thee with my son's mandrakes. And he lay with her that night.

17 And God hearkened unto Leah, and she conceived, and bare Jacob the fifth son.

18 And Leah said, God hath given me my hire, because I have given my maiden to my husband: and she called his name Issachar.

19 And Leah conceived again, and bare Jacob the sixth son.

20 And Leah said, God hath endued me *with* a good dowry; now will my husband dwell with me, because I have borne him six sons: and she called his name Zebulun.

21 And afterwards she bare a daughter, and called her name Dinah.

22 And God remembered Rachel, and God hearkened to her, and opened her womb.

23 And she conceived, and bare a son; and said, God hath taken away my reproach.

24 And she called his name Joseph; and said, T e LORD shall add to me another son.

25 And it came to pass, when Rachel had borne Joseph, that Jacob said unto Laban, Send me a ay, that I may go unto mine own place, and to y country.

26 Give *me* my wives and my children, for whom I have served thee, and let me go: for thou knowest my service which I have done thee.

27 And Laban said unto him, I pray thee, if I

have found favor in thine eyes, *tarry: for* I have learned by experience that the LORD hath blessed me for thy sake.

28 And he said, Appoint me thy wages, and I will give *it.*

29 And he said unto him, Thou knowest how I have served thee, and how thy cattle was with me.

30 For *it was* little which thou hadst before I *came,* and it is *now* increased unto a multitude; and the LORD hath blessed thee since my coming: and now, when shall I provide for mine own house also?

31 And he said, What shall I give thee? And Jacob said, Thou shalt not give me anything. If thou wilt do this thing for me, I will again feed *and* keep thy flock:

32 I will pass through all thy flock to-day, removing from thence all the speckled and spotted cattle, and all the brown cattle among the sheep, and the spotted and speckled among the goats: and *of such* shall be my hire.

33 So shall my righteousness answer for me in time to come, when it shall come for my hire before thy face: every one that *is* not speckled and spotted among the goats, and brown among the sheep, that shall be counted stolen with me.

34 And Laban said, Behold, I would it might be according to thy word.

35 And he removed that day the he-goats that were ring-streaked and spotted, and all the she-goats that were speckled and spotted, *and* every one that had *some* white in it, and all the brown among the sheep, and gave *them* into the hands of his sons.

36 And he set three days' journey betwixt himself and Jacob; and Jacob fed the rest of Laban's flocks.

37 And Jacob took him rods of green poplar, and of the hazel and chestnut-tree; and pilled white streaks in them, and made the white appear which *was* in the rods.

38 And he set the rods which he had pilled before the flocks in the gutters in the watering-troughs when the flocks came to drink; that they should conceive when they came to drink.

39. And the flocks conceived before the rods, and brought forth cattle ring-streaked, speckled, and spotted.

40 And Jacob did separate the lambs, and set the faces of the flocks toward the ring-streaked, and all the brown in the flock of Laban; and he put his own flocks by themselves, and put them not unto Laban's cattle.

41 And it came to pass, whensoever the stronger cattle did conceive, that Jacob laid the rods before the eyes of the cattle in the gutters, that they might conceive among the rods.

42 But when the cattle were feeble, he put *them* not in: so the feebler were Laban's, and the stronger Jacob's.

43 And the man increased exceedingly, and had much cattle, and maid-servants, and men-servants, and camels, and asses.

Chap. XXXI.

7 And your father hath deceived me, and changed my wages ten times; but God suffered him not to hurt me.

8 If he said thus, The speckled shall be thy wages: then all the cattle bare speckled: and if he said thus, The ring-streaked shall be thy hire; then bare all the cattle ring-streaked.

9 Thus God hath taken away the cattle of your father, and given *them* to me.

10 And it came to pass at the time that the cattle conceived, that I lifted up mine eyes, and saw in a dream, and, behold, the rams which leaped upon the cattle *were* ring-streaked, speckled, and grizzled.

11 And the angel of God spake unto me in a dream, *saying*, Jacob: and I said, Here *am* I.

12 And he said, Lift up now thine eyes, and see, all the rams which leap upon the cattle *are* ring-streaked, speckled, and grizzled: for I have seen all that Laban doeth unto thee.

13 I *am* the God of Beth-el, where thou anointedst the pillar, *and* where thou vowedst a vow unto me: now arise, get thee out from this land, and return unto the land of thy kindred.

17 Then Jacob rose up, and set his sons and his wives upon camels;

18 And he carried away all his cattle, and all his goods which he had gotten, the cattle of his getting, which he had gotten in Padan-aram, for to go to Isaac his father in the land of Canaan.

19 And Laban went to sheer his sheep: and Rachel had stolen the images that *were* her father's.

20 And Jacob stole away unawares to Laban the Syrian, in that he told him not that he fled.

21 So he fled with all that he had; and he rose up and passed over the river, and set his face *toward* the mount Gilead.

22 And it was told Laban on the third day, that Jacob was fled.

23 And he took his brethren with him, and pursued after him seven days' journey: and they overtook him in the mount Gilead.

24 And God came to Laban the Syrian in a dream by night, and said unto him, Take heed that thou speak not to Jacob either good or bad.

25 Then Laban overtook Jacob. Now Jacob

had pitched his tent in the mount: and Laban
with his brethren pitched in the mount of Gilead.

26 And Laban said to Jacob, What hast thou
done, that thou hast stolen away unawares to me,
and carried away my daughters, as captives *taken*
with the sword?

31 And Jacob answered and said to Laban, Because I was afraid: for I said, Peradventure thou
wouldest take by force thy daughters from me.

32 With whomsoever thou findest thy gods, let
him not live: before our brethren discern thou
what *is* thine with me, and take *it* to thee. For
Jacob knew not that Rachel had stolen them.

33 And Laban went into Jacob's tent, and into
Leah's tent, and into the two maid-servant's tents;
but he found *them* not. Then went he out of
Leah's tent, and entered into Rachel's tent.

34 Now Rachel had taken the images, and put
them in the camel's furniture, and sat upon them.
And Laban searched all the tent, but found *them*
not.

35 And she said to her father, Let it not displease my lord that I cannot rise up before thee;
for the custom of women *is* upon me. And he
searched, but found not the images.

36 And Jacob was wroth, and chode with Laban: and Jacob answered and said to Laban, What
is my trespass? what *is* my sin, that thou hast so
hotly pursued after me?

37 Whereas thou hast searched all my stuff,
what hast thou found of all thy household stuff?
set *it* here before my brethren and thy brethren,
that they may judge betwixt us both.

38 This twenty years *have* I *been* with thee; thy
ewes and she-goats have not cast their young, and
the rams of thy flock have I not eaten.

Chap. XXXIII.

5 Who *are* those with thee? And he said, The children which God hath graciously given thy servant.

Chap. XXXIV.

1 And Dinah the daughter of Leah, which she bare unto Jacob, went out to see the daughters of the land.

2 And when Shechem the son of Hamor the Hivite, prince of the country, saw her, he took her, and lay with her, and defiled her.

3 And his soul clave unto Dinah the daughter of Jacob, and he loved the damsel, and spake kindly unto the damsel.

4 And Shechem spoke unto his father Hamor, saying, Get me this damsel to wife.

5 And Jacob heard that he had defiled Dinah his daughter: (now his sons were with his cattle in the field: and Jacob held his peace until they were come.)

6 And Hamor the father of Shechem went out unto Jacob to commune with him.

7 And the sons of Jacob came out of the field when they heard *it:* and the men were grieved and they were very wroth, because he had wrought folly in Israel, in lying with Jacob's daughter; which thing ought not to be done.

8 And Hamor communed with them, saying, The soul of my son Shechem longeth for your daughter: I pray you give her him to wife.

9 And make ye marriages with us, *and* give your daughters unto us, and take our daughters unto you.

10 And ye shall dwell with us: and the land shall be before you; dwell and trade ye therein, and get you possessions therein.

11 And Shechem said unto her father, and unto her brethren, Let me find grace in your eyes, and what ye shall say unto me, I will give.

12 Ask me never so much dowry and gift, and I will give according as ye shall say unto me: but give me the damsel to wife.

13 And the sons of Jacob answered Shechem and Hamor his father deceitfully, and said, Because he had defiled Dinah their sister:

14 And they said unto them, We cannot do this thing, to give our sister to one that is uncircumcised: for that *were* a reproach unto us:

15 But in this will we consent unto you: If ye will be as we *be*, that every male of you be circumcised;

16 Then will we give our daughters unto you, and we will take your daughters to us, and we will dwell with you, and we will become one people.

17 But if ye will not hearken unto us, to be circumcised; then will we take our daughter, and we will be gone.

18 And their words pleased Hamor, and Shechem, Hamor's son.

19 And the young man deferred not to do the thing, because he had delight in Jacob's daughter: and he *was* more honorable than all the house of his father.

20 And Hamor and Shechem his son came unto the gate of their city, and communed with the men of their city, saying,

21 These men *are* peaceable with us, therefore let them dwell in the land, and trade therein: for the land, behold, *it is* large enough for them: let us take their daughters to us for wives, and let us give them our daughters.

22 Only herein will the men consent unto us for to dwell with us, to be one people, if every male

among us be circumcised, as they *are* circumcised.

23 *Shall* not their cattle, and their substance, and every beast of theirs *be* ours? only let us consent unto them, and they will dwell with us.

24 And unto Hamor, and unto Shechem his son, hearkened all that went out of the gate of his city : and every male was circumcised, all that went out of the gate of his city.

25 And it came to pass on the third day, when they were sore, that two of the sons of Jacob, Simeon and Levi, Dinah's brethren took each man his sword, and came upon the city boldly, and slew all the males.

26 And they slew Hamor and Shechem his son with the edge of the sword, and took Dinah out of Shechem's house, and went out.

27 The sons of Jacob came upon the slain, and spoiled the city ; because they had defiled their sister.

28 They took their sheep, and their oxen, and their asses, and that which *was* in the city, and that which *was* in the field.

29 And all their wealth and all their little ones, and their wives took they captive, and spoiled even all that *was* in the house.

30 And Jacob said to Simeon and Levi, Ye have troubled me to make me to stink among the inhabitants of the land, among the Canaanites, and the Perizzites : and I *being* few in number, they shall gather themselves together against me, and slay me, and I shall be destroyed, I and my house.

31 And they said, Should he deal with our sister as with an harlot?

Chap. XXXV.

11 And God said unto him, I *am* God Almighty : be fruitful and multiply ; a nation and a company

of nations shall be of thee, and kings shall come out of thy loins.

16 And they journeyed from Bethel; and there was but a little way to come to Ephrath: and Rachel travailed, and she had hard labor.

17 And it came to pass, when she was in hard labor, that the midwife said unto her, Fear not; thou shalt have this son also.

22 And it came to pass, when Israel dwelt in that land, that Reuben went and lay with Bilhah his father's concubine: and Israel heard *it.*

Chap. XXXVI.

12 And Timna was concubine to Eliphaz Esau's son; and she bare to Eliphaz, Amalek.

Chap. XXXVIII.

1. And it came to pass at that time, that Judah went down from his brethren, and turned in to a certain Adullamite, whose name *was* Hirah.

2 And Judah saw there a daughter of a certain Canaanite, whose name *was* Shuah; and he took her, and went in unto her.

3 And she conceived, and bare a son; and he called his name Er.

4 And she conceived again, and bare a son; and she called his name Onan.

5 And she yet again conceived and bare a son; and called his name Shelah: and he was at Chezib, when she bare him.

6 And Judah took a wife for Er his first-born, whose name *was* Tamar.

7 And Er, Judah's first-born, was wicked in the sight of the LORD; and the LORD slew him.

8 And Judah said unto Onan, Go in unto thy brother's wife, and marry her, and raise up seed to thy brother.

9 And Onan knew that the seed should not be

his : and it came to pass, when he went in unto his brother's wife, that he spilled *it* on the ground, lest that he should give seed to his brother.

10 And the thing which he did displeased the LORD : wherefore he slew him also.

11 Then said Judah to Tamar, his daughter-in-law, Remain a widow at thy father's house, till Shelah my son be grown ; (for he said, Lest peradventure he die also as his brethren *did :*) and Tamar went and dwelt in her father's house.

12 And in process of time, the daughter of Shuah, Judah's wife died : and Judah was comforted, and went up unto his sheep-shearers to Timnath, he and his friend Hirah the Adullamite.

13 And it was told Tamar, saying, Behold, thy father-in-law goeth up to Timnath, to shear his sheep.

· 14 And she put her widow's garments off from her, and covered her with a vail, and wrapped herself, and sat in an open place, which *is* by the way to Timnath : for she saw that Shelah was grown, and she was not given unto him to wife.

15 When Judah saw her, he thought her *to be* a harlot ; because she had covered her face.

16 And he turned unto her by the way, and said, Go to, I pray thee, let me come in unto thee ; (for he knew not that she *was* his daughter-in-law :) and she said, What wilt thou give me, that thou mayest come in unto me ?

17 And he said, I will send *thee* a kid from the flock : and she said, Wilt thou give *me* a pledge till thou send *it?*

18 And he said, What pledge shall I give thee ? and she said, Thy signet, and thy bracelets, and thy staff that *is* in thy hand : and he gave *it* her, and came in unto her, and she conceived by him.

19 And she arose and went away and laid by

her vail from her, and put on the garments of her widowhood.

20 And Judah sent the kid by the hand of his friend the Adullamite, to receive *his* pledge from the woman's hand: but he found her not.

21. Then he asked the men of that place, saying, Where *is* the harlot that *was* openly by the wayside? And they said, There was no harlot in this *place.*

22 And he returned to Judah, and said, I cannot find her; and also the men of the place said, *that* there was no harlot in this *place.*

23 And Judah said, Let her take *it* to her, lest we be shamed: behold, I sent this kid, and thou hast not found her.

24 And it came to pass about three months after, that it was told Judah, saying, Tamar thy daughter-in-law hath played the harlot; and also, behold, she *is* with child by whoredom. And Judah said, Bring her forth, and let her be burnt.

25 When she *was* brought forth, she sent to her father-in-law, saying, By the man whose these *are, am* I with child: and she said, Discern, I pray thee, whose *are* these, the signet, and bracelets, and staff.

26 And Judah acknowledged *them,* and said, She hath been more righteous than I; because that I gave her not to Shelah my son: and he knew her again no more.

27 And it came to pass in the time of her travail, that behold, twins *were* in her womb.

28 And it came to pass when she travailed, that *the one* put out *his* hand; and the midwife took and bound upon his hand a scarlet thread, saying, This came out first.

29 And it came to pass as he drew back his hand, that behold, his brother came out: and she

said, How hast thou broken forth? *this* breach *be* upon thee: therefore his name was called Pharez.

30 And afterward came out his brother that had the scarlet thread upon his hand; and his name was called Zarah.

Chap. XXXIX.

7 And it came to pass after these things, that his master's wife cast her eyes upon Joseph: and she said, Lie with me.

8 But he refused, and said unto his master's wife, Behold, my master wotteth not what *is* with me in the house, and he hath committed all that he hath to my hand.

9 *There is* none greater in this house than I; neither hath he kept back any thing from me, but thee, because thou *art* his wife: how then can I do this great wickedness, and sin against God?

10 And it came to pass, as she spake to Joseph day by day, that he hearkened not unto her, to lie by her, *or* to be with her.

11 And it came to pass about this time, that *Joseph* went into the house to do his business; and *there* was none of the men of the house there within.

12 And she caught him by his garment, saying, Lie with me: and he left his garment in her hand, and fled, and got him out.

13 And it came to pass, when she saw that he had left his garment in her hand, and was fled forth,

14 That she called unto the men of her house, and spake unto them, saying, See, he hath brought in an Hebrew unto us to mock us: he came in unto me to lie with me and I cried with a loud voice:

15 And it came to pass, when he heard that I lifted up my voice and cried, that he left his garment with me, and fled, and got him out.

16 And she laid up his garment by her, until his lord came home.

17 And she spake unto him according to these words, saying, The Hebrew servant which thou hast brought unto us, came in unto me to mock me:

18 And it came to pass as I lifted up my voice and cried, that he left his garment with me, and fled out.

19 And it came to pass, when his master heard the words of his wife, which she spake unto him, saying, After this manner did thy servant to me; that his wrath was kindled.

20 And Joseph's master took him, and put him into the prison, a place where the king's prisoners *were* bound: and he was there in the prison.

Chap. XLVI.

26 All the souls that came with Jacob into Egypt, which came out of his loins, besides Jacob's sons' wives, all the souls *were* three-score and six.

Chap. XLIX.

3 Reuben, thou *art* my first-born, my might, and the beginning of my strength, the excellency of dignity, and the excellency of power:

4 Unstable as water, thou shalt not excel; because thou wentest up to thy father's bed; then defiledst thou *it:* he went up to my couch.

25 *Even* by the God of thy father, who shall help thee, and by the Almighty, who shall bless thee with blessings of heaven above, blessings of the deep that lieth under, blessings of the breasts and of the womb.

EXODUS.

Chap. I.

15 And the king of Egypt spake to the Hebrew midwives (of which the name of one *was* Shiphrah, and the name of the other Puah;)

16 And he said, When ye do the office of a midwife to the Hebrew women, and see *them* upon the stools; if it *be* a son, then ye shall kill him; but if it *be* a daughter, then she shall live.

17 But the midwives feared God, and did not as the king of Egypt commanded them, but saved the men-children alive.

18 And the king of Egypt called for the midwives, and said unto them, Why have ye done this thing, and have saved the men-children alive?

19 And the midwives said unto Pharaoh, Because the Hebrew women *are* not as the Egyptian women; for they *are* lively, and are delivered ere the midwives come in unto them.

20 Therefore God dealt well with the midwives: and the people multiplied, and waxed very mighty.

21 And it came to pass, because the midwives feared God, that he made them houses.

22 And Pharaoh charged all his people, saying, Every son that is born ye shall cast into the river, and every daughter ye shall save alive.

Chap. II.

1 And there went a man of the house of Levi, and took *to wife* a daughter of Levi.

2 And the woman conceived and bare a son: and when she saw him that he *was* a goodly *child*, she hid him three months.

Chap. IV.

25 Then Zipporah took a sharp stone, **and cut**

off the foreskin of her son, and cast *it* at his feet, and said, Surely a bloody husband *art* thou to me.

26 So he let him go: then she said, A bloody husband *thou art*, because of the circumcision.

Chap. XII.

43 And the LORD said unto Moses and Aaron, This *is* the ordinance of the passover: there shall no stranger eat thereof:

44 But every man's servant that is bought for money, when thou hast circumcised him, then shall he eat thereof.

45 For no uncircumcised person shall eat thereof.

Chap. XIII.

12 That thou shalt set apart unto the LORD all that openeth the matrix, and every firstling that cometh of a beast which thou hast; the male *shall be* the LORD'S.

15 And it came to pass, when Pharaoh would hardly let us go, that the LORD slew all the first-born in the land of Egypt, both the first-born of man, and the first-born of beast: therefore I sacrificed to the LORD all that openeth the matrix, being males; but all the first-born of my children I redeem.

16 And it shall be for a token upon thine hand.

Chap. XIX.

14 And Moses went down from the mount unto the people, and sanctified the people; and they washed their clothes.

15 And he said unto the people, Be ready against the third day: come not at *ycur* wives.

Chap. XX.

26 Neither shalt thou go up by steps unto mine altar, that thy nakedness be not discovered thereon.

Chap. XXI.

7 And if a man sell his daughter to be a maid-servant, she shall not go out as the men-servants do.

8 If she please not her master, who hath betrothed her to himself, then shall he let her be redeemed: to sell her unto a strange nation he shall have no power, seeing he hath dealt deceitfully with her.

9 And if he have betrothed her unto his son, he shall deal with her after the manner of daughters.

10 If he take him another *wife*, her food, her raiment, and her duty of marriage, shall he not diminish.

22 If men strive, and hurt a woman with child, so that her fruit depart *from her*, and yet no mischief follow: he shall be surely punished according as the woman's husband will lay upon him; and he shall pay as the judges *determine*.

23 And if *any* mischief follow, then thou shalt give life for life,

24 Eye for eye, tooth for tooth, hand for hand, foot for foot,

25 Burning for burning, wound for wound, stripe for stripe.

Chap. XXII.

16 And if a man entice a maid that is not betrothed, and lie with her, he shall surely endow her to be his wife.

17 If her father utterly refuse to give her unto him, he shall pay money according to the dowry of virgins.

18 Thou shalt not suffer a witch to live.

19 Whosoever lieth with a beast shall surely be put to death.

Chap. XXXIII.

20 And he said, Thou canst not see my face ; for there shall no man see me and live.

21 And the Lord said, Behold, *there is* a place by me, and thou shalt stand upon a rock :

22 And it shall come to pass, while my glory passeth by, that I will put thee in a cleft of the rock, and will cover thee with my hand while I pass by :

23 And I will take away mine hand, and thou shalt see my back parts ; but my face shall not be seen.

Chap. XXXIV.

15 Lest thou make a covenant with the inhabitants of the land, and they go a whoring after their gods, and do sacrifice unto their gods, and *one* call thee, and thou eat of his sacrifice ;

16 And thou take of their daughters unto thy sons, and their daughters go a whoring after their gods, and make thy sons go a whoring after their gods.

19 All that openeth the matrix *is* mine :

———

LEVITICUS.

Chap. V.

2 Or if a soul touch any unclean thing, whether *it be* a carcass of an unclean beast, or a carcass of unclean cattle, or the carcass of unclean creeping things, and *if* it be hidden from him ; he also shall be unclean, and guilty.

3 Or if he touch the uncleanness of man, whatsoever uncleanness *it be* that a man shall be defiled withal, and it be hid from him ; when he knoweth *of it*, then he shall be guilty.

Chap. XII.

1 And the Lord spake unto Moses, saying,

2 Speak unto the children of Israel, saying, If a woman have conceived seed, and borne a man-child, then she shall be unclean seven days: according to the days of the separation for her infirmity shall she be unclean.

3 And in the eighth day the flesh of his fore-skin shall be circumcised.

4 And she shall then continue in the blood of her purifying three and thirty days: she shall touch no hallowed thing, nor come into the sanctuary, until the days of her purifying be fulfilled.

5 But if she bear a maid-child, then she shall be unclean two weeks, as in her separation: and she shall continue in the blood of her purifying three-score and six days.

6 And when the days of her purifying are fulfilled, for a son, or for a daughter, she shall bring a lamb of the first year for a burnt-offering, and a young pigeon, or a turtle-dove, for a sin-offering, unto the door of the tabernacle of the congregation, unto the priest:

7 Who shall offer it before the Lord, and make an atonement for her; and she shall be cleansed from the issue of her blood. This *is* the law for her that hath borne a male or a female.

8 And if she be not able to bring a lamb, then she shall bring two turtles, or two young pigeons; the one for the burnt-offering, and the other for a sin-offering: and the priest shall make an atonement for her, and she shall be clean.

Chap. XV.

16 And if any man's seed of copulation go out from him, then he shall wash all his flesh in water, and be unclean until the even.

17 And every garment, and every skin whereon is the seed of copulation, shall be washed with water, and be unclean until the even.

18 The woman also with whom man shall lie *with* seed of copulation, they *shall* both bathe *themselves* in water, and be unclean until the even.

19 And if a woman have an issue, *and* her issue in her flesh be blood, she shall be put apart seven days: and whosoever toucheth her shall be unclean until the even.

20 And everything that she lieth upon in her separation shall be unclean: every thing also that she sitteth upon shall be unclean.

21 And whosoever toucheth her bed shall wash his clothes, and bathe *himself* in water, and be unclean until the even.

22 And whosoever toucheth any thing that she sat upon shall wash his clothes, and bathe *himself* in water, and be unclean until the even.

23 And if it *be* on *her* bed, or on any thing whereon she sitteth, when he toucheth it he shall be unclean until the even.

24 And if any man lie with her at all, and her flowers be upon him, he shall be unclean seven days: and all the bed whereon he lieth shall be unclean.

25 And if a woman have an issue of her blood many days out of the time of her separation, or if it run beyond the time of her separation; all the days of the issue of her uncleanness shall be as the days of her separation; she *shall* be unclean.

26 Every bed whereon she lieth all the days of her issue shall be unto her as the bed of her separation: and whatsoever she sitteth upon shall be unclean, as the uncleanness of her separation.

27 And whosoever toucheth those things shall be unclean, and shall wash his clothes, and bathe *himself* in water, and be unclean until the even.

31 Thus shall ye separate the children of Israel from their uncleanness: that they die not in their uncleanness, when they defile my tabernacle that *is* among them.

32 This is the law of him that hath an issue, and *of him* whose seed goeth from him, and is defiled therewith ;

33 And of her that is sick of her flowers, and of him that hath an issue, of the man, and of the woman, and of him that lieth with her that is unclean.

Chap. XVIII.

6 None of you shall approach to any that is near of kin to him, to uncover *their* nakedness ; I *am* the Lord.

7 The nakedness of thy father, or the nakedness of thy mother, shalt thou not uncover : she *is* thy mother, thou shalt not uncover her nakedness.

8 The nakedness of thy father's wife shalt thou not uncover : it is thy father's nakedness.

9 The nakedness of thy sister, the daughter of thy father, or daughter of thy mother, *whether she be* born at home, or born abroad, *even* their nakedness thou shalt not uncover.

10 The nakedness of thy son's daughter, or of thy daughter's daughter, *even* their nakedness thou shalt not uncover : for theirs *is* thine own nakedness.

11 The nakedness of thy father's wife's daughter, begotten of thy father, (she *is* thy sister,) thou shalt not uncover her nakedness.

12 Thou shalt not uncover the nakedness of thy father's sister : she is thy father's near kinswoman.

13 Thou shalt not uncover the nakedness of thy mother's sister : for she *is* thy mother's near kinswoman.

14 Thou shalt not uncover the nakedness of thy

father's brother, thou shalt not approach to his wife : she *is* thine aunt.

15 Thou shalt not uncover the nakedness of thy daughter-in-law : she *is* thy son's wife, thou shalt not uncover her nakedness.

16 Thou shalt not uncover the nakedness of thy brother's wife : it *is* thy brother's nakedness.

17 Thou shalt not uncover the nakedness of a woman and her daughter, neither shalt thou take her son's daughter, or her daughter's daughter, to uncover her nakedness, *for* they *are* her near kins- women : it *is* wickedness.

18 Neither shalt thou take a wife to her sister, to vex *her*, to uncover her nakedness, besides the other in her life-*time*.

19 Also thou shalt not approach unto a woman to uncover her nakedness, as long as she is put apart for her uncleanness.

20 Moreover, thou shalt not lie carnally with thy neighbor's wife, to defile thyself with her.

21 And thou shalt not let any of thy seed pass through *the fire* to Molech, neither shalt thou pro- fane the name of thy God : I *am* the LORD.

22 Thou shalt not lie with mankind, as with womankind : it *is* abomination.

23 Neither shalt thou lie with any beast to defile thyself therewith : neither shall any woman stand before a beast to lie down thereto : it *is* confusion.

28 That the land spew not you out also, when ye defile it, as it spewed out the nations that *were* before you.

Chap. XIX.

19 Ye shall keep my statutes. Thou shalt not let thy cattle gender with a diverse kind.

29 Do not prostitute thy daughter, to cause her to be a whore ; lest the land fall to whoredom, and the land become full of wickedness.

Chap. XX.

4 And if the people of the land do any ways hide their eyes from the man, when he giveth of his seed unto Molech, and kill him not:

5 Then I will set my face against that man, and against his family, and will cut him off, and all that go a whoring after him, to commit whoredom with Molech, from among their people.

6 And the soul that turneth after such as have familiar spirits, and after wizards, to go a whoring after them, I will even set my face against that soul, and will cut him off from among his people.

10 And the man that committeth adultery with *another* man's wife, *even he* that committeth adultery with his neighbor's wife, the adulterer and the adulteress shall surely be put to death.

11 And the man that lieth with his father's wife hath uncovered his father's nakedness: both of them shall surely be put to death: their blood *shall be* upon them.

12 And if a man lie with his daughter-in-law, both of them shall surely be put to death: they have wrought confusion; their blood *shall be* upon them.

13 If a man also lie with mankind, as he lieth with a woman, both of them have committed an abomination: they shall surely be put to death; their blood *shall be* upon them.

14 And if a man take a wife and her mother, it *is* wickedness: they shall be burnt with fire, both he and they: that there be no wickedness among you.

15 And if a man lie with a beast, he shall surely be put to death: and ye shall slay the beast.

16 And if a woman approach unto any beast, and lie down thereto, thou shalt kill the woman and the beast; they shall surely be put to death; their blood *shall be* upon them.

17 And if a man shall take his sister, his **father's** daughter, or his mother's daughter, and see her nakedness, and she see his nakedness: it *is* a wicked thing; and they shall be cut off in the sight of their people : he hath uncovered his sister's nakedness, he shall bear his iniquity.

18 And if a man shall lie with a woman having her sickness, and shall uncover her nakedness ; he hath discovered her fountain, and she hath uncovered the fountain of her blood : and both of them shall be cut off from among their people.

19 And thou shalt not uncover the nakedness of thy mother's sister, nor of thy father's sister; for he uncovereth his near kin : they shall bear their iniquity.

20 And if a man shall lie with his uncle's wife, he hath uncovered his uncle's nakedness : they shall bear their sin ; they shall die childless.

21 And if a man shall take his brother's wife, it *is* an unclean thing : he hath uncovered his brother's nakedness; they shall be childless.

Chap. XXI.

1 And the Lord said unto Moses, Speak unto the priests the sons of Aaron, and say unto them, There shall none be defiled for the dead among his people.

3 And for his sister a virgin, that is nigh unto him, which hath had no husband; for her may he be defiled.

7 They shall not take a wife *that is* a whore, or profane; neither shall they take a woman put away from her husband; for he *is* holy unto his God.

9 And the daughter of any priest, if she profane herself by playing the whore, she profaneth **her** father : she shall be burnt with fire.

13 And he shall take a wife in her virginity.

14 A widow, or a divorced woman, or profane, *or* a harlot, these shall he not take: but he shall take a virgin of his own people to wife.

15 Neither shall he profane his seed among his people : for I the LORD do sanctify him.

17 Speak unto Aaron, saying, Whosoever *he be* of thy seed in their generation that hath *any* blemish, let him not approach to offer the bread of his God.

18 For whatsoever man *he be* that hath a blemish, he shall not approach : a blind man, or a lame, or he that hath a flat nose, or anything superfluous.

19 Or a man that is brokenfooted, or brokenhanded,

20 Or crookbacked, or a dwarf, or that hath a blemish in his eye, or be scurvy, or scabbed, or hath his stones broken ;

21 No man that hath a blemish of the seed of Aaron the priest shall come nigh to offer the offerings of the LORD made by fire.

CHAP. XXII.

4 What man soever of the seed of Aaron *is* a leper, or hath a running issue ; he shall not eat of the holy things, until he be clean. And whoso toucheth any thing *that is* unclean *by* the dead, or a man whose seed goeth from him ;

5 Or whosoever toucheth any creeping thing, whereby he may be made unclean, or a man of whom he may take uncleanness, whatsoever uncleanness he hath ;

6 The soul which hath touched any such shall be unclean until even, and shall not eat of the holy things, unless he wash his flesh with water.

11 But if the priest buy *any* soul with his money, he shall eat of it, and he that is born in his house : they shall eat of his meat.

12 If the priest's daughter also be *married* **unto a stranger**, she may not eat of an offering of the holy things.

13 But if the priest's daughter be a widow, or divorced, and have no child, and is returned unto her father's house, as in her youth, she shall eat of her father's meat: but there shall no stranger eat thereof.

NUMBERS.

Chap. III.

12 And I, behold, I have taken the Levites from among the children of Israel, instead of all the first-born that openeth the matrix among the children of Israel: therefore the Levites shall be mine;

13 Because all the first-born *are* mine; *for* on the day that I smote all the first-born in the land of Egypt, I hallowed unto me all the first-born in Israel, both man and beast; mine they shall be: I *am* the LORD.

Chap. V.

11 And the LORD spake unto Moses, saying,

12 Speak unto the children of Israel, and say unto them, If any man's wife go aside, and commit a trespass against him,

13 And a man lie with her carnally, and it be hid from the eyes of her husband, and be kept close, and she be defiled, and *there be* no witness against her, neither she be taken *with the manner ;*

14 And the spirit of jealousy come upon him, and he be jealous of his wife, and she be defiled: or if the spirit of jealousy come upon him, and he be jealous of his wife, and she be not defiled:

15 Then shall the man bring his wife unto the

priest, and he shall bring her offering for her, the tenth *part* of an ephah of barley-meal; he shall pour no oil upon it, nor put frankincense thereon; for *it is* an offering of jealousy, an offering of memorial, bringing iniquity to remembrance.

16 And the priest shall bring her near, and set her before the LORD:

17 And the priest shall take holy water in an earthen vessel; and of the dust that is in the floor of the tabernacle the priest shall take, and put *it* into the water:

18 And the priest shall set the woman before the LORD, and uncover the woman's head, and put the offering of memorial in her hands, which *is* the jealousy-offering: and the priest shall have in his hand the bitter water that causeth the curse:

19 And the priest shall charge her by an oath, and say unto the woman, If no man have lain with thee, and if thou hast not gone aside to uncleanness *with another* instead of thy husband, be thou free from this bitter water that causeth the curse:

20 But if thou hast gone aside *to another* instead of thy husband, and if thou be defiled, and some man have lain with thee besides thy husband:

21 Then the priest shall charge the woman with an oath of cursing, and the priest shall say unto the woman, The LORD make thee a curse and an oath among thy people, when the LORD doth make thy thigh to rot, and thy belly to swell;

22 And this water that causeth the curse shall go into thy bowels, to make *thy* belly to swell, and *thy* thigh to rot. And the woman shall say, Amen, amen.

23 And the priest shall write these curses in a book, and he shall blot *them* out with the bitter water:

24 And he shall cause the woman to drink the bitter water that causeth the curse: and the water

that causeth the curse shall enter into her, *and be come* bitter.

25 Then the priest shall take the jealousy-offering out of the woman's hand, and shall wave the offering before the LORD, and offer it upon the altar:

26 And the priest shall take a handful of the offering, *even* the memorial thereof, and burn *it* upon the altar, and afterward shall cause the woman to drink the water.

27 And when he hath made her to drink the water, then it shall come to pass, *that*, if she be defiled, and have done trespass against her husband, that the water that causeth the curse shall enter into her, *and become* bitter, and her belly shall swell, and her thigh shall rot: and the woman shall be a curse among her people.

28 And if the woman be not defiled, but be clean; then she shall be free, and shall conceive seed.

29 This *is* the law of jealousies, when a wife goeth aside *to another* instead of her husband, and is defiled;

30 Or when the spirit of jealousy cometh upon him, and he be jealous over his wife, and shall set the woman before the LORD, and the priest shall execute upon her all this law.

31 Then shall the man be guiltless from iniquity, and this woman shall bear her iniquity.

CHAP. VIII.

16 For they [the Levites] *are* wholly given unto me from among the children of Israel; instead of such as open every womb, *even instead of* the first-born of all the children of Israel, have I taken them unto me.

17 For all the first-born of the children of Israel *are* mine, *both* man and beast: on the day that I

smote every first-born in the land of Egypt I sanctified them for myself.

18 And I have taken the Levites for all the first-born of the children of Israel.

Chap. XI.

11 And Moses said unto the Lord, Wherefore hast thou afflicted thy servant? and wherefore have I not found favor in thy sight, that thou layest the burden of all this people upon me?

12 Have I conceived all this people? have I begotten them, that thou shouldest say unto me, Carry them in thy bosom, as a nursing-father beareth the sucking child, unto the land which thou swarest unto their fathers?

Chap. XII.

9 And the anger of the Lord was kindled against them ; and he departed.

10 And the cloud departed from off the tabernacle ; and behold, Miriam *became* leprous, *white* as snow : and Aaron looked upon Miriam, and behold, *she was* leprous.

11 And Aaron said unto Moses, Alas, my lord, I beseech thee, lay not the sin upon us, wherein we have done foolishly, and wherein we have sinned.

12 Let her not be as one dead, of whom the flesh is half consumed when he cometh out of his mother's womb.

13 And Moses cried unto the Lord, saying, Heal her now, O God, I beseech thee.

14 And the Lord said unto Moses, If her father had but spit in her face, should she not be ashamed seven days? let her be shut ou* from the camp seven days, and after that let her be received in *again.*

Chap. XXV.

1 And Israel abode in Shittim, and the people

began to commit whoredom with the daughters of Moab.

4 And the LORD said unto Moses, Take all the heads of the people, and hang them up before the LORD against the sun, that the fierce anger of the LORD may be turned away from Israel.

CHAP. XXXI.

1 And the Lord spake unto Moses, saying,

2 Avenge the children of Israel of the Midianites: afterward shalt thou be gathered unto thy people.

7 And they warred against the Midianites, as the LORD commanded Moses; and they slew all the males.

8 And they slew the kings of Midian, besides the rest of them that were slain; *namely*, Evi, and Rekem, and Zur, and Hur, and Reba, five kings of Midian: Balaam also the son of Beor they slew with the sword.

9 And the children of Israel took *all* the women of Midian captives, and their little ones, and took the spoil of all their cattle, and all their flocks, and all their goods.

10 And they burnt all their cities wherein they dwelt, and all their goodly castles, with fire.

11 And they took all the spoil, and all the prey, *both* of men and of beasts.

12 And they brought the captives, and the prey, and the spoil unto Moses and Eleazar the priest, and unto the congregation of the children of Israel, unto the camp at the plains of Moab, which *are* by Jordan *near* Jericho.

13 And Moses, and Eleazar the priest, and all the princes of the congregation, went forth to meet them without the camp.

14 And Moses was wroth with the officers of the host, *with* the captains over thousands, and captains over hundreds, which came from the battle.

15 And Moses said unto them, Have ye saved all the women alive?

16 Behold, these caused the children of Israel, through the counsel of Balaam, to commit trespass against the LORD in the matter of Peor, and there was a plague among the congregation of the LORD.

17 Now therefore kill every male among the little ones, and kill every woman that hath known man by lying with him.

18 But all the women-children, that have not known a man by lying with him, keep alive for yourselves.

19 And do ye abide without the camp seven days: whosoever hath killed any person, and whosoever hath touched any slain, purify *both* yourselves and your captives on the third day, and on the seventh day.

20 And purify all *your* raiment, and all that is made of skins, and all work of goats' *hair*, and all things made of wood.

21 And Eleazar the priest said unto the men of war which went to the battle, This *is* the ordinance of the law which the LORD commanded Moses.

25 And the LORD spake unto Moses, saying,

26 Take the sum of the prey that was taken, *both* of man and of beast, thou, and Eleazar the priest, and the chief fathers of the congregation:

27 And divide the prey into two parts; between them that took the war upon them, who went out to battle, and between all the congregation:

28 And levy a tribute unto the LORD of the men of war which went out to battle.

31 And Moses and Eleazar the priest did as the LORD commanded Moses.

. **32** And the booty, *being* the rest of the prey which the men of war had caught, was six hundred thousand, and seventy thousand, and five thousand sheep,

33 And threescore and twelve thousand beeves,

34 And threescore and one thousand asses,

35 And thirty and two thousand persons in all, of women that had not known man by lying with him.

40 And the persons *were* sixteen thousand, of which the LORD'S tribute *was* thirty and two persons.

41 And Moses gave the tribute, *which was* the LORD'S heave-offering, unto Eleazar the priest; as the LORD commanded Moses.

47 Even of the children of Israel's half, Moses took one portion of fifty, *both* of man and of beast, and gave them unto the Levites, which kept the charge of the tabernacle of the LORD; as the LORD commanded Moses.

DEUTERONOMY.

CHAP. XX.

10 When thou comest nigh unto a city to fight against it, then proclaim peace unto it.

13 And when the LORD thy God hath delivered it into thine hands, thou shalt smite every male thereof with the edge of the sword:

14 But the women, and the little ones, and the cattle, and all that is in the city, *even* all the spoil thereof, shalt thou take unto thyself: and thou shalt eat the spoil of thine enemies, which the LORD thy God hath given thee.

15 Thus shalt thou do unto all the cities *which*

are very far off from thee, which *are* not of the cities of these nations.

16 But of the cities of these people, which the LORD thy God doth give thee *for* an inheritance, thou shall save alive nothing that breatheth :

CHAP. XXI.

10 When thou goest forth to war against thine enemies, and the LORD thy God hath delivered them into thine hands, and thou hast taken them captive,

11 And seest among the captives a beautiful woman, and hast a desire unto her, that thou wouldest have her to thy wife;

12 Then thou shalt bring her home to thine house; and she shall shave her head, and pare her nails;

13 And she shall put the raiment of her captivity from off her, and shall remain in thine house, and bewail her father and her mother a full month : and after that thou shalt go in unto her, and be her husband, and she shall be thy wife.

14 And it shall be, if thou have no delight in her, then thou shalt let her go whither she will; but thou shalt not sell her at all for money, thou shalt not make merchandise of her, because thou hast humbled her.

15 If a man have two wives, one beloved, and another hated, and they have borne him children, *both* the beloved and the hated; and *if* the first-born son be hers that was hated :

16 Then it shall be, when he maketh his sons to inherit *that* which he hath, *that* he may not make the son of the beloved first-born before the son of the hated, *which is indeed* the first-born :

17 But he shall acknowledge the son of the hated *for* the first-born, by giving him a double

portion of all that he hath : for he *is* the beginning of his strength ; the right of the first-born *is* his.

Chap. XXII.

13 If any man take a wife, and go in unto her, and hate her,

14 And give occasions of speech against her, and bring up an evil name upon her, and say, I took this woman, and when I came to her, I found her not a maid :

15 Then shall the father of the damsel, and her mother, take and bring forth *the tokens of* the damsel's virginity unto the elders of the city in the gate :

16 And the damsel's father shall say unto the elders, I gave my daughter unto this man to wife, and he hateth her,

17 And, lo, he hath given occasions of speech *against her*, saying, I found not thy daughter a maid ; and yet these *are the tokens of* my daughter's virginity. And they shall spread the cloth before the elders of the city.

18 And the elders of that city shall take that man, and chastise him ;

19 And they shall amerce him in an hundred *shekels* of silver, and give *them* unto the father of the damsel, because he hath brought up an evil name upon a virgin of Israel : and she shall be his wife ; he may not put her away all his days.

20 But if this thing be true, *and the tokens of* virginity be not found for the damsel :

21 Then they shall bring out the damsel to the door of her father's house, and the men of her city shall stone her with stones that she die ; because she hath wrought folly in Israel, to play the whore in her father's house : so shalt thou put evil away from among you.

22 If a man be found lying with a woman married to a husband, then they shall both of them die, *both* the man that lay with the woman, and the woman : so shalt thou put away evil from Israel.

23 If a damsel *that is* a virgin be betrothed unto a husband, and a man find her in the city, and lie with her;

24 Then ye shall bring them both out unto the gate of that city, and ye shall stone them with stones that they die; the damsel, because she cried not, *being* in the city; and the man, because he hath humbled his neighbor's wife: so thou shalt put away evil from among you.

25 But if a man find a betrothed damsel in the field, and the man force her, and lie with her; then the man only that lay with her shall die:

26 But unto the damsel thou shalt do nothing, *there is* in the damsel no sin *worthy* of death : for as when a man riseth against his neighbor, and slayeth him, even so *is* this matter :

27 For he found her in the field, *and* the betrothed damsel cried, and *there was* none to save her.

28 If a man find a damsel *that is* a virgin, which is not betrothed, and lay hold on her, and lie with her, and they be found;

29 Then the man that lay with her shall give unto the damsel's father fifty *shekels* of silver, and she shall be his wife; because he hath humbled her, he may not put her away all his days.

30 A man shall not take his father's wife, nor discover his father's skirt.

CHAP. XXIII.

1 He that is wounded in the stones, or hath his privy member cut off, shall not enter into the congregation of the LORD.

2 A bastard shall not enter into the congregation of the LORD; even to his tenth generation shall he not enter into the congregation of the LORD.

10 If there be among you any man that is not clean by reason of uncleanness that chanceth him by night, then shall he go abroad out of the camp, he shall not come within the camp:

11 But it shall be, when evening cometh on, he shall wash *himself* with water: and when the sun is down, he shall come into the camp again.

12 Thou shalt have a place also without the camp, wither thou shalt go forth abroad:

13 And thou shalt have a paddle upon thy weapon: and it shall be, when thou wilt ease thyself abroad, thou shalt dig therewith, and shalt turn back and cover that which cometh from thee:

14 For the LORD thy God walketh in the midst of thy camp, to deliver thee, and to give up thine enemies before thee ; therefore shall thy camp be holy: that he see no unclean thing in thee, and turn away from thee.

17 There shall be no whore of the daughters of Israel, nor a sodomite of the sons of Israel.

18 Thou shalt not bring the hire of a whore, or the price of a dog, into the house of the LORD thy God for any vow: for even both these *are* abomination unto the LORD thy God.

CHAP. XXIV.

1 When a man hath taken a wife, and married her, and it come to pass that she find no favor in his eyes, because he hath found some uncleanness in her : then let him write her a bill of divorcement, and give *it* in her hand, and send her out of his house.

2 And when she is departed out of his house, she may go and be another man's *wife.*

3 And *if* the latter husband hate her, and write her a bill of divorcement, and giveth *it* in her hand, and sendeth her out of his house ; or if the latter husband die, which took her *to be* his wife ;

4 Her former husband, which sent her away, may not take her again to be his wife, after that she is defiled ; for that *is* abomination before the LORD : and thou shalt not cause the land to sin, which the LORD thy God giveth thee *for* an inheritance.

5 When a man hath taken a new wife, he shall not go out to war, neither shall he be charged with any business: *but* he shall be free at home one year, and shall cheer up his wife which he hath taken.

CHAP. XXV.

5 If brethren dwell together, and one of them die, and have no child, the wife of the dead shall not marry without unto a stranger: her husband's brother shall go in unto her, and take her to him to wife, and perform the duty of a husband's brother unto her.

6 And it shall be, *that* the first-born which she beareth shall succeed in the name of his brother *which is* dead, that his name be not put out of Israel.

7 And if the man like not to take his brother's wife, then let his brother's wife go up to the gate unto the elders, and say, My husband's brother refuseth to raise up unto his brother a name in Israel, he will not perform the duty of my husband's brother.

8 Then the elders of his city shall call him, and speak unto him : and *if* he stand *to it,* and say, I like not to take her;

9 Then shall his brother's wife come unto him in the presence of the elders, and loose his shoe from off his foot, and spit in his face, and shall **an**

swer and say, So shall it be done unto that man that will not build up his brother's house.

10 And his name shall be called in Israel, The house of him that hath his shoe loosed.

11 When men strive together one with another, and the wife of the one draweth near for to deliver her husband out of the hand of him that smiteth him, and putteth forth her hand, and taketh him by the secrets;

12 Then thou shalt cut off her hand, thine eye shall not pity *her.*

Chap. XXVII.

20 Cursed *be* he that lieth with his father's wife; because he uncovereth his father's skirt:

21 Cursed *be* he that lieth with any manner of beast:

22 Cursed *be* he that lieth with his sister, the daughter of his father, or the daughter of his mother:

23 Cursed *be* he that lieth with his mother-in-law. And all the people shall say, Amen.

Chap. XXVIII.

4 Blessed *shall be* the fruit of thy body, and the fruit of thy ground, and the fruit of thy cattle, the increase of thy kine, and the flocks of thy sheep.

13 And the LORD shall make thee the head, and not the tail; and thou shalt be above only, and and thou shalt not be beneath.

27 The LORD will smite thee with the botch of Egypt, and with the emerods, and with the scab, and with the itch, whereof thou canst not be healed.

30 Thou shalt betroth a wife, and another man shall lie with her.

35 The LORD shall smite thee in the knees, and in the legs, with a sore botch that cannot be healed,

from the sole of thy foot unto the top of thy head.

56 The tender and delicate woman among you, which would not adventure to set the sole of her foot upon the ground for delicateness and tenderness, her eye shall be evil toward the husband of her bosom, and toward her son, and toward her daughter,

57 And toward her young one that cometh out between her feet, and toward her children which she shall bear.

JOSHUA.

Chap. II.

1 And Joshua the son of Nun sent out of Shittim two men to spy secretly, saying, Go view the land, even Jericho. And they went, and came into a harlot's house, named Rahab, and lodged there.

15 Then she let them down by a cord through the window :

16 And she said unto them, Get you to the mountain, lest the pursuers meet you.

18 Behold, *when* we come into the land, thou shalt bind this line of scarlet thread in the window which thou didst let us down by :

21 And she sent them away, and they departed ; and she bound the scarlet line in the window.

Chap. V.

2 At that time the LORD said unto Joshua, Make thee sharp knives, and circumcise again the children of Israel the second time.

3 And Joshua made him sharp knives, and cir-

cumcised the children of Israel at the hill of the foreskins.

4 And this *is* the cause why Joshua did circumcise: All the people that came out of Egypt, *that were* males, *even* all the men of war died in the wilderness by the way, after they came out of Egypt.

5 Now all the people that came out were circumcised; but all the people *that were* born in the wilderness by the way as they came forth out of Egypt, *them* they had not circumcised.

Chap. VI.

1 Now Jericho was straitly shut up, because of the chilren of Israel:

2 And the LORD said unto Joshua, . . . seven priests shall bear before the ark seven trumpets of rams' horns: and the seventh day ye shall compass the city seven times, and the priests shall blow with the trumpets.

17 And the city shall be accursed, *even* it, and all that *are* therein, to the LORD: only Rahab the harlot shall live, she and all that *are* with her in the house, because she hid the messengers that we sent.

20 So the people shouted when *the priests* blew with the trumpets: and it came to pass, when the people heard the sound of the trumpet, and the people shouted with a great shout, that the wall fell down flat, so that the people went up into the city, every man straight before him, and they took the city.

21 And they utterly destroyed all that *was* in the city, both man and woman, young and old, and ox, and sheep, and ass, with the edge of the sword.

23 And the young men that were spies went in, and brought out Rahab, and her father, and her

mother, and her brethren, and all that she had; and they brought out all her kindred, and left them without the camp of Israel.

25 And Joshua saved Rahab the harlot alive, and her father's household, and all that she had; and she dwelleth in Israel *even* unto this day; because she hid the messengers which Joshua sent to spy out Jericho.

———

JUDGES.

Chap. III.

21 And Ehud put forth his left hand, and took the dagger from his right thigh, and thrust it into his belly:

22 And the haft also went in after the blade: and the fat closed upon the blade, so that he could not draw the dagger out of his belly; and the dirt came out.

Chap. XI.

1 Now Jephthah the Gileadite was a mighty man of valor, and he *was* the son of a harlot: and Gilead begat Jephthah.

2 And Gilead's wife bare him sons; and his wife's sons grew up, and they thrust out Jephthah, and said unto him, Thou shalt not inherit in our father's house; for thou *art* the son of a strange woman.

30 And Jephthah vowed a vow unto the LORD, and said, If thou shalt without fail deliver the children of Ammon into mine hands,

31 Then it shall be, that whatsoever cometh forth of the doors of my house to meet me, when I return in peace from the children of Ammon, shall surely be the LORD'S, and I will offer it up for a burnt-offering.

32 So Jephthah passed over unto the children of Ammon to fight against them: and the LORD delivered them into his hands.

34 And Jephthah came to Mizpeh unto his house, and behold, his daughter came out to meet him with timbrels and with dances: and she *was his* only child; besides her he had neither son nor daughter.

35 And it came to pass, when he saw her, that he rent his clothes, and said, Alas, my daughter! thou hast brought me very low, and thou art one of them that trouble me: for I have opened my mouth unto the LORD, and I cannot go back.

37 And she said unto her father, Let this thing be done for me: Let me alone two months, that I may go up and down upon the mountains, and bewail my virginity, I and my fellows.

38 And he said, Go. And he sent her away *for* two months: and she went with her companions, and bewailed her virginity upon the mountains.

39 And it came to pass, at the end of two months, that she returned unto her father, who did with her *according* to his vow which he had vowed: and she knew no man.

CHAP. XIII.

2 And there was a certain man of Zorah, of the family of the Danites, whose name *was* Manoah; and his wife *was* barren, and bare not.

3 And the angel of the LORD appeared unto the woman, and said unto her, Behold now, thou *art* barren and bearest not: but thou shalt conceive, and bear a son.

4 Now therefore beware, I pray thee, and drink not wine nor strong drink, and eat not any unclean *thing:*

5 For, lo, thou shalt conceive, and bear a son;

and no razor shall come on his head : for the child shall be a Nazarite unto God from the womb; and he shall begin to deliver Israel out of the hand of the Philistines.

9 And God hearkened to the voice of Manoah; and the angel of God came again unto the woman as she sat in the field : but Manoah her husband *was* not with her.

24 And the woman bare a son, and called his name Samson : and the child grew, and the LORD blessed him.

25 And the Spirit of the LORD began to move him at times in the camp of Dan, between Zorah and Eshtaol.

CHAP. XV.

1 But it came to pass within a while after, in the time of wheat-harvest, that Samson visited his wife with a kid : and he said, I will go in to my wife into the chamber : but her father would not suffer him to go in.

2 And her father said, I verily thought that thou hadst utterly hated her : therefore I gave her to thy companion : *is* not her younger sister fairer than she? take her, I pray thee, instead of her.

4 And Samson went and caught three hundred foxes, and took fire-brands, and turned tail to tail, and put a fire-brand in the midst between two tails.

5 And when he had set the brands on fire, he let *them* go into the standing corn of the Philistines, and burnt up both the shocks, and also the standing corn, with the vineyard *and* olives.

15 And he found a new jaw-bone of an ass, and put forth his hand, and took it, and slew a thousand men therewith.

16 And Samson said, With the jaw-bone of an ass, heaps upon heaps, with the jaw of an ass have I slain a thousand men.

18 And he was sore athirst, and called on **the**
Lord, and said, Thou hast given this great deliverance into the hand of thy servant: and now shall
I die for thirst, and fall into the hand of the uncircumcised?

19 But God clave a hollow place that *was* in
the jaw, and there came water thereout; and when
he had drunk, his spirit came again, and he re-
vived. Wherefore he called the name thereof
En-hakkore, which *is* in Lehi unto this day.

20 And he judged Israel in the days of the
Philistines twenty years.

Chap. XVI.

1 Then went Samson to Gaza, and saw there an
harlot, and went in unto her.

3 And Samson lay till midnight, and arose at
midnight, and took the doors of the gate of the
city, and the two posts, and went away with them,
bar and all, and put *them* upon his shoulders, and
carried them up to the top of a hill that is before
Hebron.

4 And it came to pass afterward, that he loved
a woman in the valley of Sorek, whose name *was*
Delilah.

5 And the lords of the Philistines came up unto
her, and said unto her, Entice him, and see wherein his great strength *lieth*, and by what *means* we
may prevail against him, that we may bind him to
afflict him: and we will give thee every one of us
eleven hundred *pieces* of silver.

16 And it came to pass, when she pressed him
daily with her words, and urged him, *so* that his
soul was vexed unto death;

17 That he told her all his heart, and said unto
her, There hath not come a razor upon mine head:
for I *have been* a Nazarite unto God from my moth-

er's womb : if I be shaven, then my strength will go from me, and I shall become weak, and be like any *other* man.

19 And she made him sleep upon her knees; and she called for a man, and she caused him to shave off the seven locks of his head; and she began to afflict him, and his strength went from him.

CHAP. XIX.

1 And it came to pass in those days, when *there was* no king in Israel, that there was a certain Levite sojourning on the side of mount Ephraim, who took to him a concubine out of Beth-lehem-judah.

2 And his concubine played the whore against him, and went away from him unto her father's house to Beth-lehem-judah, and was there four whole months.

3 And her husband arose, and went after her.

9 And when the man rose up to depart, he, and his concubine, and his servant, his father-in-law, the damsel's father, said unto him, Behold, now the day draweth toward evening, I pray you tarry all night.

10 But the man would not tarry that night, but he rose up and departed, and came over against Jebus, which *is* Jerusalem : and *there were* with him two asses saddled, his concubine also *was* with him.

15 And they turned aside thither, to go in *and* to lodge in Gibeah : and when he went in, he sat him down in a street of the city : for *there was* no man that took them into his house to lodging.

16 And behold, there came an old man from his work out of the field at even, which *was* also of mount Ephraim ; and he sojourned in Gibeah ; but the men of the place *were* Benjamites.

20 And the old man said, Peace *be* with thee·

howsoever, *let* all thy wants *lie* upon me; only lodge not in the street.

21 So he brought him into his house, and gave provender unto the asses: and they washed their feet, and did eat and drink.

22 *Now* as they were making their hearts merry, behold, the men of the city, certain sons of Belial, beset the house round about, *and* beat at the door, and spake to the master of the house, the old man, saying, Bring forth the man that came into thine house, that we may know him.

23 And the man, the master of the house, went out unto them, and said unto them, Nay, my brethren, *nay*, I pray you, do not *so* wickedly; seeing that this man is come into mine house, do not this folly.

24 Behold, *here is* my daughter, a maiden, and his concubine; them I will bring out now, and humble ye them, and do with them what seemeth good unto you: but unto this man do not so vile a thing.

25 But the men would not hearken to him: so the man took his concubine, and brought her forth unto them; and they knew her, and abused her all the night until the morning: and when the day began to spring they let her go. •

26 Then came the woman in the dawning of the day, and fell down at the door of the man's house where her lord *was*, till it was light.

27 And her lord rose up in the morning, and opened the doors of the house, and went out to go his way: and, behold, the woman his concubine was fallen down *at* the door of the house, and her hands *were* upon the threshold.

28 And he said unto her, Up, and let us be going. But none answered. Then the man took her *up* upon an ass, and the man rose up, and gat him unto his place.

29 And when he was come into his house, he took a knife, and laid hold on his concubine, and divided her, *together* with her bones, into twelve pieces, and sent her into all the coasts of Israel.

30 And it was so, that all that saw it, said, There was no such deed done nor seen from the day that the children of Israel came up out of the land of Egypt unto this day: consider of it, take advice, and speak *your minds*.

CHAP. XX.

3 (Now the children of Benjamin heard that the children of Israel were gone up to Mizpeh.) Then said the children of Israel, Tell *us*, how was this wickedness?

4 And the Levite, the husband of the woman that was slain, answered and said, I came into Gibeah that *belongeth* to Benjamin, I and my concubine, to lodge.

5 And the men of Gibeah rose against me, and beset the house round about upon me by night, *and* thought to have slain me: *and* my concubine have they forced, that she is dead.

6 And I took my concubine, and cut her in pieces, and sent her throughout all the country of the inheritance of Israel: for they have committed lewdness and folly in Israel.

8 And all the people arose as one man, saying, We will not any *of us* go to his tent, neither will we any *of us* turn into his house.

13 But the children of Benjamin would not hearken to the voice of their brethren the children of Israel:

14 But the children of Benjamin gathered themselves together out of the cities unto Gibeah, to go out to battle against the children of Israel.

35 And the LORD smote Benjamin before Israel:

and the children of Israel destroyed of the Benjamites that day twenty and five thousand and an hundred men : all these drew the sword.

47 But six hundred men turned and fled to the wilderness unto the rock Rimmon, and abode in the rock Rimmon four months.

Chap. XXI.

1 Now the men of Israel had sworn in Mizpeh, saying, There shall not any of us give his daughter unto Benjamin to wife.

6 And the children of Israel repented them for Benjamin their brother, and said, There is one tribe cut off from Israel this day.

7 How shall we do for wives for them that remain, seeing we have sworn by the LORD, that we will not give them of our daughters to wives ?

10 And the congregation sent thither twelve thousand men of the valiantest, and commanded them, saying, Go and smite the inhabitants of Jabesh-gilead with the edge of the sword, with the women and the children.

11 And this *is* the thing that ye shall do, Ye shall utterly destroy every male, and every woman that hath lain by man.

12 And they found among the inhabitants of Jabesh-gilead four hundred young virgins, that had known no man by lying with any male : and they brought them unto the camp to Shiloh, which *is* in the land of Canaan.

13 And the whole congregation sent *some* to speak to the children of Benjamin that *were* in the rock Rimmon, and to call peaceably unto them.

14 And Benjamin came again at that time ; and they gave them wives which they had saved alive of the women of Jabesh-gilead : and yet so they sufficed them not.

16 Then the elders of the congregation said, How shall we do for wives for them that remain, seeing the women are destroyed out of Benjamin?

17 And they said, *There must be* an inheritance for them that be escaped of Benjamin, that a tribe be not destroyed out of Israel.

18 Howbeit we may not give them wives of our daughters: for the children of Israel have sworn, saying, Cursed *be* he that giveth a wife to Benjamin.

19 Then they said, Behold, *there is* a feast of the LORD in Shiloh yearly, *in a place* which *is* on the north side of Beth-el, on the east side of the highway that goeth up from Beth-el to Shechem, and on the south of Lebonah.

20 Therefore they commanded the children of Benjamin, saying, Go and lie in wait in the vineyards;

21 And see, and, behold, if the daughters of Shiloh come out to dance in dances, then come ye out of the vineyards, and catch you every man his wife of the daughters of Shiloh, and go to the land of Benjamin.

22 And it shall be, when their fathers or their brethren come unto us to complain, that we will say unto them, Be favorable unto them for our sakes: because we reserved not to each man his wife in the war: for ye did not give unto them at this time, *that* ye should be guilty.

23 And the children of Benjamin did so, and took *them* wives, according to their number, of them that danced, whom they caught: and they went and returned unto their inheritance, and repaired the cities, and dwelt in them.

RUTH.

Chap. I.

11 And Naomi said, Turn again, my daughters : why will ye go with me? *are* there yet *any more* sons in my womb, that they may be your husbands?

12 Turn again, my daughters, go *your way;* for I am too old to have a husband. If I should say, I have hope, *if* I should have a husband also to-night, and should also bear sons;

13 Would ye tarry for them till they were grown? would ye stay for them from having husbands? nay, my daughters :

14 And Orpah kissed her mother-in-law; but Ruth clave unto her.

Chap. III.

1 Then Naomi her mother-in-law said unto her, My daughter, shall I not seek rest for thee, that it may be well with thee?

2 And now *is* not Boaz of our kindred, with whose maidens thou wast? Behold, he winnoweth barley to-night in the threshing-floor.

3 Wash thyself therefore, and anoint thee, and put thy raiment upon thee, and get thee down to the floor : *but* make not thyself known unto the man, until he shall have done eating and drinking.

4 And it shall be when he lieth down, that thou shalt mark the place where he shall lie, and thou shalt go in, and uncover his feet, and lay thee down; and he will tell thee what thou shalt do.

5 And she said unto her, All that thou sayest unto me I will do.

6 And she went down unto the floor, and did according to all that her mother-in-law bade her.

7 And when Boaz had eaten and drunk, and his heart was merry, he went to lie down at the end of the heap of corn: and she came softly, and uncovered his feet, and laid her down.

8 And it came to pass at midnight, that the man was afraid, and turned himself: and behold, a woman lay at his feet.

9 And he said, Who *art* thou? And she answered, I *am* Ruth thine handmaid: spread therefore thy skirt over thine handmaid; for thou *art* a near kinsman.

10 And he said, blessed *be* thou of the LORD, my daughter: *for* thou hast shewed more kindness in the latter end than at the beginning, inasmuch as thou followedst not young men, whether poor or rich.

11 And now, my daughter, fear not; I will do to thee all that thou requirest: for all the city of my people doth know that thou *art* a virtuous woman.

13 Tarry this night: . . . lie down until the morning.

14 And she lay at his feet until the morning: and she rose up before one could know another. And he said, Let it not be known that a woman came into the floor.

15 Also he said, Bring the vail that *thou hast* upon thee, and hold it. And when she held it, he measured six *measures* of barley, and laid *it* on her: and she went into the city.

16 And when she came to her mother-in-law, she said, Who *art* thou, my daughter? and she told her all that the man had done to her.

CHAP. IV.

9 And Boaz said unto the elders, and *unto* all the people,

10 Moreover, Ruth the Moabitess, the **wife of** Mahlon, have I purchased to be my wife.

11 And all the people that *were* in the gate, and the elders, said, *We are* witnesses. The LORD make the woman that is come into thine house like Rachel and like Leah, which two did build the house of Israel: and do thou worthily. in Ephratah, and be famous in Beth-lehem:

12 And let thy house be like the house of Pharez, whom Tamar bare unto Judah, of the seed which the LORD shall give thee of this young woman.

13 So Boaz took Ruth, and she was his wife: and when he went in unto her, the LORD gave her conception and she bare a son.

17 And the women her neighbors gave it a name, saying, There is a son born to Naomi; and they called his name Obed: he *is* the father of Jesse, the father of David.

I. SAMUEL.

CHAP. I.

1 Now there was a certain man of mount Eph-raim, and his name *was* Elkanah:

2 And he had two wives; the name of the one *was* Hannah, and the name of the other Peninnah: and Peninnah had children, but Hannah had no children.

4 And when the time was that Elkanah offered, he gave to Peninnah his wife, and to all her sons and her daughters, portions:

5 But unto Hannah he gave a worthy portion; for he loved Hannah: but the LORD had shut up her womb.

16 And her adversary also provoked her sore, for to make her fret, because the LORD had shut up her womb.

7 And *as* he did so year by year, when she went up to the house of the LORD, so she provoked her, therefore she wept, and did not eat.

8 Then said Elkanah her husband to her, Hannah, why weepest thou? and why eatest thou not? and why is thy heart grieved? *am* not I better to thee than ten sons?

9 So Hannah rose up after they had eaten in Shiloh, and after they had drunk. (Now Eli the priest sat upon a seat by a post of the temple of the LORD.)

10 And she *was* in bitterness of soul, and prayed unto the LORD, and wept sore.

11 And she vowed a vow, and said, O LORD of hosts, if thou wilt indeed look on the affliction of thine handmaid, and remember me, and not forget thine handmaid, but will give unto thine handmaid a man-child, then I will give him unto the LORD all the days of his life, and there shall no razor come upon his head.

17 Then Eli answered and said, Go in peace: and the God of Israel grant *thee* thy petition that thou hast asked of him.

18 And she said, Let thine handmaid find grace in thy sight. So the woman went her way, and did eat, and her countenance was no more *sad*.

19 And they rose up in the morning early, and worshiped before the LORD, and returned, and came to their house to Ramah; and Elkanah knew Hannah his wife; and the LORD remembered her.

20 Wherefore it came to pass, when the time was come about after Hannah had conceived, that she bare a son, and called his name Samuel, *saying*, Because I have asked him of the LORD.

23 And Elkanah her husband said unto her, Do what seemeth thee good; tarry until thou have weaned him; only the LORD establish his word. So the woman abode, and gave her son suck until she weaned him.

CHAP. II.

20 And Eli blessed Elkanah and his wife, and said, The LORD give thee seed of this woman for the loan which is lent to the LORD.

21 And the LORD visited Hannah, so that she conceived, and bare three sons and two daughters. And the child Samuel grew before the LORD.

22 Now Eli was very old, and heard all that his sons did unto all Israel; and how they lay with the women that assembled *at* the door of the tabernacle of the congregation.

CHAP. IV.

19 And his daughter-in-law, Phinehas' wife, was with child *near* to be delivered: and when she heard the tidings that the ark of God was taken, and that her father-in-law and her husband were dead, she bowed herself, and travailed; for her pains came upon her.

20 And about the time of her death, the women that stood by her said unto her, Fear not, for thou hast borne a son. But she answered not, neither did she regard *it.*

CHAP. V.

6 But the hand of the LORD was heavy upon them of Ashdod, and he destroyed them, and smote them with emerods.

7 And when the men of Ashdod saw that *it was* so, they said, The ark of the God of Israel shall not abide with us.

8 Let the ark of the God of Israel be carried

about unto Gath. And they carried the ark of the God of Israel about *thither*.

9 And it was *so*, that after they had carried it about, the hand of the LORD was against the city with a very great destruction: and he smote the men of the city both small and great, and they had emerods in their secret parts.

CHAP. VI.

4 Then said they, What *shall be* the trespass offering which we shall return to him? They answered, Five golden emerods and five golden mice, *according to* the number of the lords of the Philistines: for one plague *was* on you all, and on your lords.

5 Wherefore ye shall make images of your emerods, and images of your mice that mar the land.

CHAP. XVIII.

17 And Saul said to David, Behold, mine elder daughter Merab, her will I give thee to wife.

19 But it came to pass at the time when Merab, Saul's daughter, should have been given to David, that she was given unto Adriel the Meholathite to wife.

20 And Michal, Saul's daughter, loved David: and they told Saul, and the thing pleased him.

21 And Saul said, I will give him her, that she may be a snare to him, and that the hand of the Philistines may be against him. Wherefore Saul said to David, Thou shalt this day be my son-in-law, in *the one of* the twain.

25 And Saul said, Thus shall ye say to David, the king desireth not any dowry, but a hundred foreskins of the Philistines, to be avenged of the king's enemies. But Saul thought to make David fall by the hand of the Philistines.

27 Wherefore David arose and went, he and his

men, and slew of the Philistines two hundred **men**; and David brought their foreskins, and they gave them in full tale to the king, that he might be the king's son-in-law. And Saul gave him Michal his daughter to wife.

Chap. XIX.

23 And he [Saul] went thither to Naioth in Ramah: and the Spirit of God was upon him also, and he went on, and prophesied, until he came to Naioth in Ramah.

24 And he stripped off his clothes also, and prophesied before Samuel in like manner, and lay down naked all that day and all that night.

Chap. XX.

30 Then Saul's anger was kindled against Jonathan, and he said unto him, Thou son of the perverse rebellious *woman*, do not I know that thou hast chosen the son of Jesse to thine own confusion, and unto the confusion of thy mother's nakedness?

Chap. XXI.

4 And the priest answered David, and said, *There is* no common bread under mine hand, but there is hallowed bread; if the young men have kept themselves at least from women.

5 And David answered the priest, and said unto him, Of a truth women *have been* kept from us about these three days, since I came out, and the vessels of the young men are holy, and *the bread is* in a manner common, yea, though it were sanctified this day in the vessel.

6 So the priest gave him hallowed *bread.*

13 And he [David] changed his behavior before them, and feigned himself mad in their hands, and scrabbled on the doors of the gate, and let his spittle fall down upon his beard.

Chap. XXV.

3 Now the name of the man *was* Nabal; and the name of his wife Abigail: and *she was* a woman of good understanding, and of a beautiful countenance: but the man *was* churlish and evil in his doings.

14 But one of the young men told Abigail, Nabal's wife, saying, Behold, David sent messengers out of the wilderness to salute our master; and he railed on them.

18 Then Abigail made haste, and took two hundred loaves, and two bottles of wine, and five sheep ready dressed, and five measures of parched *corn*, and a hundred clusters of raisins, and two hundred cakes of figs and laid *them* on asses.

19 And she said unto her servants, Go on before me; behold, I come after you. But she told not her husband Nabal.

22 (So and more also do God unto the enemies of David, if I leave of all that *pertain* to him by the morning light any that pisseth against the wall.)

23 And when Abigail saw David, she hasted, and lighted off the ass, and fell before David on her face, and bowed herself to the ground.

32 And David said to Abigail, Blessed *be* the LORD God of Israel, which sent thee this day to meet me:

34 For in very deed, *as* the LORD God of Israel liveth, which hath kept me back from hurting thee, except thou hadst hasted and come to meet me, surely there had not been left unto Nabal by the morning light any that pisseth against the wall.

35 So David received of her hand *that* which she had brought him, and said unto her, Go up in peace to thine house; see, I have harkened to thy voice, and have accepted thy person.

38 And it came to pass about ten days *after*, that the Lord smote Nabal, that he died.

39 And when David heard that Nabal was dead, he said, Blessed *be* the Lord, that hath pleaded the cause of my reproach from the hand of Nabal, and hath kept his servant from evil: for the Lord hath returned the wickedness of Nabal upon his own head. And David sent and communed with Abigail, to take her to him to wife.

40 And when the servants of David were come to Abigail to Carmel, they spake unto her, saying, David sent us unto thee, to take thee to him to wife.

41 And she arose, and bowed herself on *her* face to the earth, and said, Behold, *let* thine handmaid *be* a servant to wash the feet of the servants of my lord.

42 And Abigail hasted, and arose, and rode upon an ass, with five damsels of hers that went after her; and she went after the messengers of David, and became his wife.

43 David also took Ahinoam of Jezreel; and they were also both of them his wives.

44 But Saul had given Michal his daughter, David's wife, to Phalti the son of Laish, which *was* of Gallim.

II. SAMUEL.

Chap. III.

7 And Saul had a concubine, whose name *was* Rizpah, the daughter of Aiah : and *Ish-bosheth* said to Abner, Wherefore hast thou gone in unto my father's concubine?

8 Then was Abner very wroth for the words of

Ish-bosheth, and said, *Am* I a dog's head, which against Judah do shew kindness this day unto the house of Saul thy father, to his brethren, and to his friends, and have not delivered thee into the hand of David, that thou chargest me to-day with a fault concerning this woman?

13 And he [David] said, Well; I will make a league with thee: but one thing I require of thee, that is, Thou shalt not see my face, except thou first bring Michal, Saul's daughter, when thou comest to see my face.

14 And David sent messengers to Ish-bosheth, Saul's son, saying, Deliver *me* my wife Michal, which I espoused to me for an hundred foreskins of the Philistines.

15 And Ish-bosheth sent, and took her from *her* husband, *even* from Phaltiel the son of Laish.

16 And her husband went with her along weeping behind her to Bahurim. Then said Abner unto him, Go, return. And he returned.

CHAP. V.

13 And David took *him* more concubines and wives out of Jerusalem, after he was come from Hebron: and there were yet sons and daughters born to David.

CHAP. VI.

14 And David danced before the LORD with all *his* might; and David *was* girded with a linen ephod.

16 And as the ark of the LORD came into the city of David, Michal, Saul's daughter, looked through a window, and saw king David leaping and dancing before the LORD; and she despised him in her heart.

20 Then David returned to bless his household. And Michal the daughter of Saul came out to meet

David, and said, How glorious was the king of Israel to-day, who uncovered himself to-day in the eyes of the handmaids of his servants, as one of the vain fellows shamelessly uncovereth himself!

21 And David said unto Michal, *It was* before the LORD, which chose me before thy father, and before all his house, to appoint me ruler over the people of the Lord, over Israel: therefore will I play before the LORD.

22 And I will yet be more vile than thus, and will be base in mine own sight: and of the maid-servants which thou hast spoken of, of them shall I be had in honor.

23 Therefore Michal the daughter of Saul had no child unto the day of her death.

CHAP. X.

4 Wherefore Hanun took David's servants, and shaved off the one half of their beards, and cut off their garments in the middle, *even* to their buttocks, and sent them away.

5 When they told *it* unto David, he sent to meet them, because the men were greatly ashamed: and the king said, Tarry at Jericho until your beards be grown, and *then* return.

6 And when the children of Ammon saw that they stank before David, the children of Ammon sent and hired the Syrians.

CHAP. XI.

2 And it came to pass in an eveningtide, that David arose from off his bed, and walked upon the roof of the king's house: and from the roof he saw a woman washing herself; and the woman *was* very beautiful to look upon.

3 And David sent and inquired after the woman. And *one* said, *Is* not this Bath-sheba, the daughter of Eliam, the wife of Uriah the Hittite?

4 And David sent messengers and took her; and she came in unto him, and he lay with her; for she was purified from her uncleanness: and she returned unto her house.

5 And the woman conceived, and sent and told David, and said, I *am* with child.

6 And David sent to Joab, *saying*, Send me Uriah the Hittite. And Joab sent Uriah to David.

7 And when Uriah was come unto him, David demanded *of him* how Joab did, and how the people did, and how the war prospered.

8 And David said to Uriah, Go down to thy house, and wash thy feet. And Uriah departed out of the king's house, and there followed him a mess *of meat* from the king.

9 But Uriah slept at the door of the king's house with all the servants of his lord, and went not down to his house.

10 And when they had told David, saying, Uriah went not down unto his house, David said unto Uriah, camest thou not from *thy* journey? why *then* didst thou not go down unto thine house?

11 And Uriah said unto David, The ark and Israel, and Judah, abide in tents; and my lord Joab, and the servants of my lord, are encamped in the open fields; shall I then go into mine house, to eat and to drink, and to lie with my wife? *As* thou livest, and *as* thy soul liveth, I will not do this thing.

12 And David said to Uriah, Tarry here to-day also, and to-morrow I will let thee depart. So Uriah abode in Jerusalem that day and the morrow.

13 And when David had called him, he did eat and drink before him; and he made him drunk: and at even he went out to lie on his bed with the

servants of his lord, but went not down to his house.

14 And it came to pass in the morning, that David wrote a letter to Joab, and sent *it* by the hand of Uriah.

15 And he wrote in the letter, saying, Set ye Uriah in the forefront of the hottest battle, and retire ye from him, that he may be smitten, and die.

16 And it came to pass, when Joab observed the city, that he assigned Uriah unto a place where he knew that valiant men *were.*

17 And the men of the city went out, and fought with Joab: and there fell *some* of the people of the servants of David; and Uriah the Hittite died also.

18 Then Joab sent and told David all the things concerning the war;

19 And charged the messenger, saying, When thou hast made an end of telling the matters of the war unto the king, . . then say thou, Thy servant Uriah the Hittite is dead also.

22 So the messenger went, and came and showed David all that Joab had sent him for.

25 Then David said unto the messenger, Thus shalt thou say unto Joab, Let not this thing displease thee, for the sword devoureth one as well as another: make thy battle more strong against the city, and overthrow it: and encourage thou him.

26 And when the wife of Uriah heard that Uriah her husband was dead, she mourned for her husband.

27 And when the mourning was past, David sent and fetched her to his house, and she became his wife, and bare him a son. But the thing that David had done displeased the LORD.

Chap. XII.

1 And the Lord sent Nathan unto David. And he came unto him, and said unto him, There were two men in one city ; the one rich, and the other poor.

2 The rich *man* had exceeding many flocks and herds :

3 But the poor *man* had nothing save one little ewe-lamb, which he had bought and nourished up : and it grew up together with him, and with his children ; it did eat of his own meat, and drank of his own cup, and lay in his bosom, and was unto him as a daughter.

4 And there came a traveller unto the rich man, and he spared to take of his own flock and of his own herd, to dress for the wayfaring man that was come unto him ; but took the poor man's lamb, and dressed it for the man that was come to him.

5 And David's anger was greatly kindled against the man ; and he said to Nathan, *As* the Lord liveth, the man that hath done this *thing* shall surely die.

6 And he shall restore the lamb four-fold, because he did this thing, and because he had no pity,

7 And Nathan said to David, Thou *art* the man. Thus saith the Lord God of Israel, I anointed thee king over Israel, and I delivered thee out of the hand of Saul ;

8 And I gave thee thy master's house, and thy master's wives into thy bosom, and gave thee the house of Israel and of Judah ; and if *that had been* too little, I would moreover have given unto thee such and such things.

9 Wherefore hast thou despised the commandment of the Lord, to do evil in his sight? thou

hast killed Uriah the Hittite with the sword, and hast taken his wife *to be* thy wife, and hast slain him with the sword of the children of Ammon.

10 Now therefore the sword shall never depart from thine house; because thou hast despised me, and hast taken the wife of Uriah the Hittite to be thy wife.

11 Thus saith the LORD, Behold, I will raise up evil against thee out of thine own house, and I will take thy wives before thine eyes, and give *them* unto thy neighbor, and he shall lie with thy wives in the sight of this sun.

12 For thou didst *it* secretly: but I will do this thing before all Israel, and before the sun.

13 And David said unto Nathan, I have sinned against the LORD. And Nathan said unto David, The Lord also hath put away thy sin; thou shalt not die.

14 Howbeit, because by this deed thou hast given great occasion to the enemies of the LORD to blaspheme, the child also *that is* born unto thee shall surely die.

15 And Nathan departed unto his house. And the LORD struck the child that Uriah's wife bare unto David, and it was very sick.

18 And it came to pass on the seventh day that the child died.

24 And David comforted Bath-sheba his wife, and went in unto her, and lay with her: and she bare a son, and he called his name Solomon: and the LORD loved him.

CHAP. XIII.

1 And it came to pass after this, that Absalom the son of David had a fair sister, whose name *was* Tamar; and Amnon the son of David loved her.

2 And Amnon was so vexed, that he fell sick

for his sister Tamar; for she *was* a virgin; and Amnon thought it hard for him to do any thing to her.

3 But Amnon had a friend, whose name *was* Jonadab, the son of Shimeah David's brother: and Jonadab *was* a very subtile man.

4 And he said unto him, Why *art* thou, *being* the king's son, lean from day to day? wilt thou not tell me? And Amnon said unto him, I love Tamar, my brother Absalom's sister.

5 And Jonadab said unto him, Lay thee down on thy bed, and make thyself sick: and when thy father cometh to see thee, say unto him, I pray thee, let my sister Tamar come, and give me meat, and dress the meat in my sight, that I may see *it*, and eat *it* at her hand.

6 So Amnon lay down, and made himself sick: and when the king was come to see him, Amnon said unto the king, I pray thee, let Tamar my sister come, and make me a couple of cakes in my sight, that I may eat at her hand.

7 Then David sent home to Tamar, saying, Go now to thy brother Amnon's house, and dress him meat.

8 So Tamar went to her brother Amnon's house; and he was laid down. And she took flour and kneaded *it*, and made cakes in his sight, and did bake the cakes.

11 And when she had brought *them* unto him to eat, he took hold of her, and said unto her, Come lie with me, my sister.

12 And she answered him, Nay, my brother, do not force me; for no such thing ought to be done in Israel: do not thou this folly.

13 And I, whither shall I cause my shame to go? and as for thee, thou shalt be as one of the fools in Israel. Now therefore, I pray thee, speak

84

unto the king; for he will not withhold me from thee.

14 Howbeit he would not hearken unto her voice : but, being stronger than she, forced her, and lay with her.

15 Then Amnon hated her exceedingly ; so that the hatred wherewith he hated her *was* greater than the love wherewith he had loved her. And Amnon said unto her, Arise, be gone.

16 And she said unto him, *There is* no cause : this evil in sending me away *is* greater than the other that thou didst unto me. But he would not hearken unto her.

17 Then he called his servant that ministered unto him, and said, Put now this *woman* out from me, and bolt the door after her.

18 And *she had* a garment of divers colors upon her : for with such robes were the king's daughters *that were* virgins apparelled. Then his servant brought her out, and bolted the door after her.

19 And Tamar put ashes on her head, and rent her garment of divers colors that *was* on her, and laid her hand on her head, and went on crying.

20 And Absalom her brother said unto her, Hath Amnon thy brother been with thee? but hold now thy peace, my sister : he *is* thy brother · regard not this thing. So Tamar remained desolate in her brother Absalom's house.

21 But when king David heard of all these things, he was very wroth.

22 And Absalom spake unto his brother Amnon neither good nor bad : for Absalom hated Amnon because he had forced his sister Tamar.

30 And it came to pass, while they were in the way, that tidings came to David, saying, Absalom hath slain all the king's sons, and there is not one of them left.

32 And Jonadab, the son of Shimeah David's brother, answered and said, Let not my lord suppose *that* they have slain all the young men the king's sons; for Amnon only is dead: for by the appointment of Absalom this hath been determined from the day that he forced his sister Tamar.

Chap. XV.

16 And the king went forth, and all his household after him. And the king left ten women *which were* concubines to keep the house.

Chap. XVI.

11 And David said to Abishai, and to all his servants, Behold, my son, which came forth of my bowels, seeketh my life.

21 And Ahithophel said unto Absalom, Go in unto thy father's concubines, which he hath left to keep the house; and all Israel shall hear that thou art abhorred of thy father: then shall the hands of all that *are* with thee be strong.

22 So they spread Absalom a tent upon the top of the house; and Absalom went in unto his father's concubines in the sight of all Israel.

Chap. XIX.

5 And Joab came into the house to the king, and said, Thou hast shamed this day the faces of all thy servants, which this day have saved thy life, and the lives of thy sons and of thy daughters, and the lives of thy wives, and the lives of thy concubines;

Chap. XX.

3 And David came to his house at Jerusalem, and the king took the ten women *his* concubines, whom he had left to keep the house, and put them in ward, and fed them, but went not in unto them. So they were shut up unto the day of their death, living in widowhood.

I. KINGS.

Chap. I.

1 Now king David was old *and* stricken in years; and they covered him with clothes, but he gat no heat.

2 Wherefore his servants said unto him, Let there be sought for my lord the king a young virgin: and let her stand before the king, and let her cherish him, and let her lie in thy bosom, that my lord the king may get heat.

3 So they sought for a fair damsel throughout all the coasts of Israel, and found Abishag a Shunammite, and brought her to the king.

5 And the damsel *was* very fair, and cherished the king, and ministered to him: but the king knew her not.

Chap. X.

13 And king Solomon gave unto the queen of Sheba all her desire, whatsoever she asked, besides *that* which Solomon gave her of his royal bounty.

Chap. XI.

1 But king Solomon loved many strange women, together with the daughter of Pharaoh,

2 Of the nations *concerning* which the Lord said unto the children of Israel, Ye shall not go in to them, neither shall they come in unto you: *for* surely they will turn away your heart after their gods: Solomon clave unto these in love.

3 And he had seven hundred wives, princesses, and three hundred concubines: and his wives turned away his heart.

4 For it came to pass, when Solomon was old, *that* his wives turned away his heart after other

gods : and his heart was not perfect with the LORD his God, as *was* the heart of David his father.

8 And likewise did he for all his strange wives, which burnt incense and sacrificed unto their gods.

CHAP. XIV.

10 Therefore behold, I will bring evil upon the house of Jeroboam, and will cut off from Jeroboam him that pisseth against the wall, *and* him that is shut up and left in Israel, and will take away the remnant of the house of Jeroboam, as a man taketh away dung, till it be all gone.

CHAP. XVI.

11 And it came to pass, when he began to reign, as soon as he sat on his throne, *that* he slew all the house of Baasha : he left him not one that pisseth against a wall, neither of his kinsfolks, nor of his friends.

CHAP. XXI.

21 Behold, I will bring evil upon thee, and will take away thy posterity, and will cut off from Ahab him that pisseth against the wall.

II. KINGS.

CHAP. IV.

8 And it fell on a day, that Elisha passed to Shunem, where *was* a great woman ; and she constrained him to eat bread. And *so* it was, *that* as oft as he passed by, he turned in thither to eat bread.

9 And she said unto her husband, Behold now I perceive that this *is* a holy man of God, which passeth by us continually.

10 Let us make a little chamber, I pray thee, on

the wall ; and let us set for him there a bed, and a table, and a stool, and a candlestick : and it shall be, when he cometh to us, that he shall turn in thither.

11 And it fell on a day, that he came thither, and he turned into the chamber, and lay there.

12 And he said to Gehazi his servant, Call this Shunammite. And when he had called her, she stood before him.

13 And he said unto him, Say now unto her, Behold, thou hast been careful for us with all this care ; what *is* to be done for thee ? wouldest thou be spoken for to the king, or to the captain of the host ? And she answered, I dwell among mine own people.

14 And he said, What then *is* to be done for her ? And Gehazi answered, Verily she hath no child, and her husband is old.

15 And he said, Call her. And when he had called her, she stood in the door.

16 And he said, About this season, according to the time of life, thou shalt embrace a son. And she said, Nay, my lord, *thou* man of God, do not lie unto thine handmaid.

17 And the woman conceived, and bare a son at that season that Elisha had said unto her, according to the time of life.

Chap. IX.

8 I will cut off from Ahab him that pisseth against the wall.

10 And the dogs shall eat Jezebel in the portion of Jezreel, and *there shall be* none to bury *her*.

Chap. XX.

18 And of thy sons that shall issue from thee, which thou shalt beget, shall they take away ; and they shall be eunuchs in the palace of the king of Babylon.

Chap. XXI.

12 Therefore thus saith the Lord God of Israel, Behold, I *am* bringing *such* evil upon Jerusalem and Judah, that whosoever heareth of it, both his ears shall tingle.

13 And I will stretch over Jerusalem the line of Samaria, and the plummet of the house of Ahab: and I will wipe Jerusalem as *a man* wipeth a dish, wiping *it*, and turning *it* upside down.

I. CHRONICLES.

Chap. XIX.

4 Wherefore Hanun took David's servants, and shaved them, and cut off their garments in the midst hard by their buttocks, and sent them away.

II. CHRONICLES.

Chap. IX.

1 And when the queen of Sheba heard of the fame of Solomon, she came to prove Solomon with hard questions at Jerusalem. . . . And when she was come to Solomon, she communed with him of all that was in her heart.

2 And Solomon told her all her questions: and there was nothing hid from Solomon which he told her not.

12 And king Solomon gave to the queen of Sheba all her desire, whatsoever she asked.

Chap. XI.

18 And Rehoboam took him Mahalath the

daughter of Jerimoth the son of David to wife, *and* Abihail the daughter of Eliab the son of Jesse;

19 Which bare him children.

20 And after her he took Maachah the daughter of Absalom; which bare him Abijah, and Attai, and Ziza, and Shelomith.

21 And Rehoboam loved Maachah the daughter of Absalom above all his wives and his concubines: (for he took eighteen wives, and threescore concubines; and begat twenty and eight sons, and threescore daughters.)

Chap. XIII.

21 But Abijah waxed mighty, and married fourteen wives, and begat twenty and two sons, and sixteen daughters.

Chap. XXI.

8 In his days the Edomites revolted from under the dominion of Judah, and made themselves a king.

9 Then Jehoram . . . made high places in the mountains of Judah, and caused the inhabitants of Jerusalem to commit fornication, and compelled Judah *thereto*.

12 And there came a writing to him from Elijah the prophet, saying, Thus saith the LORD God of David thy father, Because thou . . . hast walked in the way of the kings of Israel, and hast made Judah and the inhabitants of Jerusalem to go a whoring, like to the whoredoms of the house of Ahab.

14 Behold, with a great plague will the LORD smite thy people, and thy children, and thy wives, and all thy goods:

15 And thou *shalt have* great sickness by disease of thy bowels, until thy bowels fall out by reason of the sickness day by day.

18 And after all this the LORD smote him in his bowels with an incurable disease.

19 And it came to pass, that in process of time, after the end of two years, his bowels fell out by reason of his sickness: so he died of sore diseases.

EZRA.

CHAP. X.

10 And Ezra the priest stood up, and said unto them, Ye have transgressed, and have taken strange wives to increase the trespass of Israel.

11 Now therefore make confession unto the LORD God of your fathers, and do his pleasure: and separate yourselves from the people of the land, and from the strange wives.

12 Then all the congregation answered and said with a loud voice, As thou hast said, so must we do.

14 Let now our rulers of all the congregation sta ad, and let all them which have taken strange wives in our cities come at appointed times, and with them the elders of every city, and the judges thereof, until the fierce wrath of our God for this matter be turned from us.

17 And they made an end with all the men that had taken strange wives by the first day of the first month.

18 And among the sons of the priests there were found that had taken strange wives: *namely*, of the sons of Jeshua the son of Jozadak, and his brethren; Maaseiah, and Eliezer, and Jarib, and Gedaliah.

19 And they gave their hands that they would put away their wives; and *being* guilty, *they offered* a ram of the flock for their trespass.

NEHEMIAH.

Chap. XIII.

23 In those days also saw I Jews *that* had married wives of Ashdod, of Ammon, *and* of Moab:

24 And their children spake half in the speech of Ashdod, and could not speak in the Jews' language, but according to the language of each people.

25 And I contended with them, and cursed them, and smote certain of them, and plucked off their hair, and made them swear by God, *saying*, Ye shall not give your daughters unto their sons, nor take their daughters unto your sons, or for yourselves.

26 Did not Solomon king of Israel sin by these things? yet among many nations was there no king like him, who was beloved of his God, and God made him king over all Israel: nevertheless even him did outlandish women cause to sin.

27 Shall we then hearken unto you to do all this great evil to transgress against our God in marrying strange wives?

28 And *one* of the sons of Joiada, the son of Eliashib the high priest, *was* son in law to Sanballat the Horonite: therefore I chased him from me.

ESTHER.

Chap. I.

9 Also Vashti the queen made a feast for the women *in* the royal house which *belonged* to king Ahasuerus.

10 On the seventh day, when the heart of the king was merry with wine, he commanded the seven chamberlains that served in the presence of Ahasuerus the king,

11 To bring Vashti the queen before the king with the crown royal, to show the people and the princes her beauty: for she *was* fair to look on.

12 But the queen Vashti refused to come at the king's commandment by *his* chamberlains: therefore was the king very wroth, and his anger burned in him.

16 And Memucan answered before the king and the princes, Vashti the queen hath not done wrong to the king only, but also to all the princes, and to all the people that *are* in all the provinces of the king Ahasuerus.

17 For *this* deed of the queen shall come abroad unto all women, so that they shall despise their husbands in their eyes, when it shall be reported, The king Ahasuerus commanded Vashti the queen to be brought in before him, but she came not.

19 If it please the king, let there go a royal commandment from him, and let it be written among the laws of the Persians and the Medes, that it be not altered, That Vashti come no more before king Ahasuerus; and let the king give her royal estate unto another that is better than she.

20 And when the king's decree which he shall make shall be published throughout all his empire, (for it is great,) all the wives shall give to their husbands honor, both to great and small.

21 And the saying pleased the king and the princes; and the king did according to the word of Memucan.

Chap. II.

2 Then said the king's servants that ministered

unto him, Let there be fair young virgins sought
for the king:

4 And let the maiden which pleaseth the king
be queen instead of Vashti.   And the thing pleased
the king; and he did so.

12 Now when every maid's turn was come to go
in to king Ahasuerus, after that she had been
twelve months, according to the manner of the
women, (for so were the days of their purifications
accomplished, *to wit*, six months with oil of myrrh,
and six months with sweet odors, and *other* things
for the purifying of the women,)

13 Then thus came *every* maiden unto the king;
whatsoever she desired was given her to go with
her out of the house of the women unto the king's
house.

14 In the evening she went, and on the morrow
she returned into the second house of the women,
to the custody of Shaashgaz, the king's chamber-
lain, which kept the concubines: she came in unto
the king no more, except the king delighted in her,
and that she were called by name.

17 And the king loved Esther above all the
women, and she obtained grace and favor in his
sight more than all the virgins; so that he set the
royal crown upon her head, and made her queen
instead of Vashti.

Chap. VII.

8 Then the king returned out of the palace garden into the place of the banquet of wine; and
Haman was fallen upon the bed whereon Esther
was.   Then said the king, Will he force the queen
also before me in the house?

JOB.

Chap. I.

21 Naked came I out of my mother's womb, and naked shall I return thither.

Chap. II.

7 So went Satan forth from the presence of the Lord, and smote Job with sore boils from the sole of his foot unto his crown.

8 And he took him a potsherd to scrape himself withal; and he sat down among the ashes.

Chap. III.

3 Let the day perish wherein I was born, and the night *in which* it was said, There is a man child conceived.

4 Let that day be darkness;

10 Because it shut not up the doors of my *mother's* womb, nor hid sorrow from mine eyes.

11 Why died I not from the womb? *why* did I *not* give up the ghost when I came out of the belly?

12 Why did the knees prevent me? or why the breasts that I should suck?

16 Or as a hidden untimely birth I had not been; as infants *which* never saw light.

Chap. X.

18 Wherefore then hast thou brought me forth out of the womb? Oh that I had given up the ghost, and no eye had seen me.

19 I should have been as though I had not been; I should have been carried from the womb to the grave.

Chap. XIX.

17 My breath is strange to my wife, though I

entreated for the children's *sake* of mine own body.

20 My bone cleaveth to my skin and to my flesh, and I am escaped with the skin of my teeth.

26 And *though* after my skin *worms* destroy this *body*, yet in my flesh shall I see God.

Chap. XXIV.

20 The womb shall forget him.

21 He evil entreateth the barren *that* beareth not.

Chap. XXV.

4 How can he be clean *that is* born of a wo-man?

6 How much less man, *that is* a worm; and the son of man, *which is* a worm?

Chap. XXXI.

1 I made a covenant with mine eyes; why then should I think upon a maid?

9 If mine heart have been deceived by a wo-man, or *if* I have laid wait at my neighbor's door;

10 *Then* let my wife grind unto another, and let others bow down upon her.

15 Did not he that made me in the womb make him? and did not one fashion us in the womb?

18 I have guided her from my mother's womb.

Chap. XXXIX.

1 Knowest thou the time when the wild goats of the rock bring forth; *or* canst thou mark when the hinds do calve?

2 Canst thou number the months *that* they ful-fill? or knowest thou· the time when they bring forth?

3 They bow themselves, they bring forth their young ones, they cast out their sorrows.

4 Their young ones arc in good liking.
Chap. XL.

16 Lo now, his strength *is* in his loins, and his force *is* in the navel of his belly.

17 He moveth his tail like a cedar; the sinews of his stones are wrapped together.

PSALMS.

Psalm XXXVIII.

3 *There is* no soundness in my flesh because of thine anger; neither *is there any* rest in my bones because of my sin.

5 My wounds stink, *and* are corrupt because of my foolishness.

7 For my loins are filled with a loathsome *disease:* and *there is* no soundness in my flesh.

8 I am feeble and sore broken: I have roared by reason of the disquietness of my heart.

11 My lovers and my friends stand aloof from my sore; and my kinsmen stand afar off.

Psalm XLI.

7 All that hate me whisper together against me: against me do they devise my hurt.

8 An evil disease, *say they*, cleaveth fast unto him: and *now* that he lieth he shall rise up no more.

9 Yea, mine own familiar friend, in whom I trusted, which did eat of my bread, hath lifted up *his* heel against me.

Psalm XLIV.

25 For our soul is bowed down to the dust: our belly cleaveth unto the earth.

Psalm XLVIII.

6 Fear took hold upon them there, *and* pain, **as** of a woman in travail.

Psalm LI.

5 Behold I was shapen in iniquity; and in sin did my mother conceive me.

6 Behold, thou desirest truth in the inward parts.

Psalm LVIII.

3 The wicked are estranged from the womb: they go astray as soon as they be born, speaking lies.

Psalm LXXIII.

21 Thus my heart was grieved, and I was pricked in my reins.

22 So foolish *was* I, and ignorant: I was *as* a beast before thee.

Psalm LXXVIII.

70 He chose David.

71 From following the ewes great with young he brought him to feed Jacob his people, and Israel his inheritance.

Psalm LXXXVIII.

8 Thou hast put away mine acquaintance far from me; thou hast made me an abomination unto them: *I am* shut up, and I cannot come forth.

Psalms CVI.

14 But lusted exceedingly in the wilderness, and tempted God in the desert.

37 Yea, they sacrificed their sons and their daughters unto devils.

38 And shed innocent blood, *even* the blood of their sons and of their daughters, whom they sacrificed unto the idols of Canaan: and the land was polluted with blood.

39 Thus were they defiled with their own works, and went a whoring with their own inventions.

Psalm CIX.

6 Set thou a wicked man over him: and let Satan stand at his right hand.

7 When he shall be judged, let him be condemned: and let his prayer become sin.

8 Let his days be few; *and* let another take his office.

9 Let his children be fatherless, and his wife a widow.

10 Let his children be continually vagabonds, and beg; let them seek *their bread* also out of their desolate places.

11 Let the extortioner catch all that he hath; and let the strangers spoil his labor.

12 Let there be none to extend mercy unto him: neither let there be any to favor his fatherless children.

13 Let his posterity be cut off; *and* in the generation following let their name be blotted out.

14 Let the iniquity of his fathers be remembered with the LORD; and let not the sin of his mother be blotted out.

15 Let them be before the LORD continually, that he may cut off the memory of them from the earth.

16 Because that he remembered not to shew mercy, but persecuted the poor and needy man, that he might even slay the broken in heart.

17 As he loved cursing, so let it come unto him. as he delighted not in blessing, so let it be far from him.

18 As he clothed himself with cursing like as with his garment, so let it come into his bowels like water, and like oil into his bones.

19 Let it be unto him as the garment *which* covereth him, and for a girdle wherewith he is girdled continually.

20 *Let* this *be* the reward of mine adversaries from the LORD, and of them that speak evil against my soul.

PSALM CXXVIII.

3 Thy wife *shall be* as a fruitful vine by the sides of thine house: thy children like olive plants round about thy table.

PSALM CXXXII.

11 The LORD hath sworn *in* truth unto David; he will not turn from it; Of the fruit of thy body will I set upon thy throne.

PROVERBS.

CHAP. V.

3 For the lips of a strange woman drop *as* a honeycomb, and her mouth *is* smoother than oil:

4 But her end is bitter as wormwood, sharp as a twoedged sword.

5 Her feet go down to death; her steps take hold on hell.

11 And thou mourn at the last, when thy flesh and thy body are consumed.

15 Drink waters out of thine own cistern, and running waters out of thine own well.

16 Let thy fountains be dispersed abroad, *and* rivers of waters in the streets.

17 Let them be only thine own, and not strangers' with thee.

18 Let thy fountain be blessed: and rejoice with the wife of thy youth.

19 *Let her be as* the loving hin'd and pleasant **roe;** let her breasts satisfy thee at all times; and **be** thou ravished always with her love.

20 And why wilt thou, my son, be ravished **with** a strange woman, and embrace the bosom of **a** stranger?

CHAP. VI.

24 To keep thee from the evil woman, from the flattery of the tongue of a strange woman.

25 Lust not after her beauty in thy heart; neither let her take thee with her eyelids.

26 For by means of a whorish woman *a man is brought* to a piece of bread: and the adulteress will hunt for the precious life.

27 Can a man take fire in his bosom, and his clothes not be burned?

28 Can one go upon hot coals, and his feet not be buri ed?

29 So he that goeth in to his neighbor's wife; whosoever toucheth her shall not be innocent.

32 *But* whoso committeth adultery with a woman, iacketh understanding: he *that* doeth it, destroyeth his own soul.

33 A wound and dishonor shall he get; and his reproach shall not be wiped away.

34 For jealousy *is* the rage of a man: therefore he will not spare in the day of vengeance.

35 He will not regard any ransom; neither will he rest content, though thou givest many gifts.

CHAP. VII.

5 That they may keep thee from the strange woman, from the stranger *which* flattereth with her words.

6 For at the window of my house I looked through my casement,

7 And beheld among the simple ones, I discerned among the youths, a young man void of understanding,

8 Passing through the street near her corner; and he went the way to her house,

9 In the twilight, in the evening, in the black and dark night:

10 And behold, there met him a woman *with* the attire of a harlot and subtile of heart.

11 (She *is* loud and stubborn; her feet abide not in her house:

12 Now *is she* without, now in the streets, and lieth in wait at every corner,)

13 So she caught him, and kissed him, *and* with an impudent face said unto him,

14 *I have* peace-offerings with me; this day have I paid my vows.

15 Therefore came I forth to meet thee, diligently to seek thy face, and I have found thee.

16 I have decked my bed with coverings of tapestry, with carved *works*, with fine linen of Egypt.

17 I have perfumed my bed with myrrh, aloes, and cinnamon.

18 Come, let us take our fill of love until the morning: let us solace ourselves with loves.

19 For the good-man *is* not at home, he is gone a long journey:

20 He hath taken a bag of money with him, *and* will come home at the day appointed.

21 With her much fair speech she caused him to yield, with the flattering of her lips she forced him.

22 He goeth after her straightway, as an ox goeth to the slaughter, or as a fool to the correction of the stocks;

23 Till a dart strike through his liver; as a bird hasteth to the snare, and knoweth not that it *is* for his life.

25 Let not thine heart decline to her ways, **go** not astray in her paths.

26 For she hath cast down many wounded : yea, many strong *men* have been slain by her.

27 Her house *is* the way to hell, going down **to** the chambers of death.

Chap. IX.

13 A foolish woman *is* clamorous: *she is* simple, and knoweth nothing.

14 For she sitteth at the door of her house, **on** a seat in the high places of the city,

15 To call passengers who go right on their ways:

16 Whoso *is* simple, let him turn in hither: and *as for* him that wanteth understanding, she saith **to** him,

17 Stolen waters are sweet, and bread *eaten* in secret is pleasant.

18 But he knoweth not that the dead *are* there; *and that* her guests *are* in the depths of hell.

Chap. XVIII.

8 The words of a tale-bearer *are* as wounds, and they go down into the innermost parts of the belly.

20 A man's belly shall be satisfied with the fruit of his mouth.

Chap. XX.

27 The spirit of man *is* the candle of the LORD, searching all the inward parts of the belly.

30 The blueness of a wound cleanseth away evil : so *do* stripes the inward parts of the belly.

Chap. XXIII.

27 For a whore *is* a deep ditch ; and a strange woman *is* a narrow pit.

28 She also lieth in wait as *for* a prey, and increaseth the transgressors among men.

CHAP. XXVII.

13 Take his garment that is surety for **a** stranger, and take a pledge of him for a strange woman.

CHAP. XXX.

15 There are three *things that* are never satisfied, *yea,* four *thinys* say not, *It is* enough :

16 The grave ; and the barren womb ; the earth *that* is not filled with water ; and the fire.

18 There be three *things which are* too wonderful for me, yea, four which I know not :

19 The way of an eagle in the air ; the way of a serpent upon a rock ; the way of a ship in the midst of the sea; and the way of a man with a maid.

20 Such *is* the way of an adulterous woman ; she eateth, and wipeth her mouth, and saith, I have done no wickedness.

CHAP. XXXI.

1 The words of king Lemuel, the prophecy that his mother taught him.

2 What, my son? and what, the son of my womb? and what, the son of my vows ?

3 Give not thy strength unto women, nor thy ways to that which destroyeth kings.

ECCLESIASTES.

CHAP. V.

15 As he came forth of his mother's womb, naked shall he return to go as he came.

CHAP. VII.

26 And I find more bitter than death the woman, whose heart *is* snares and nets, *and* her hands *as* bands: whoso pleaseth God shall escape from her; but the sinner shall be taken by her.

27 Behold, this have I found, saith the Preacher, *counting* one by one, to find out the account;

28 Which yet my soul seeketh, but I find not: one man among a thousand have I found; but a woman among all those have I not found.

CHAP. X.

1 Dead flies cause the ointment of the apothecary to send forth a stinking savor: *so doth* a little folly him that is in reputation for wisdom *and* honor.

THE SONG OF SOLOMON.

CHAP. I.

1 The Song of songs, which *is* Solomon's.

2 Let him kiss me with the kisses of his mouth: for thy love *is* better than wine.

3 Because of the savor of thy good ointments thy name *is as* ointment poured forth, therefore do the virgins love thee.

4 Draw me, we will run after thee: the King hath brought me into his chambers: we will be glad and rejoice in thee, we will remember thy love more than wine: the upright love thee.

5 I *am* black, but comely, O ye daughters of Jerusalem, as the tents of Kedar, as the curtains of Solomon.

6 Look not upon me, because I *am* black, because the sun hath looked upon me: my mother's children were angry with me; they made me the keeper of the vineyards; *but* mine own vineyard have I not kept.

7 Tell me, O thou whom my soul loveth, **where** thou feedest, where thou makest *thy flock* to rest at noon: for **why** should I be as one that turneth aside by the flocks of thy companions?

8 If thou know not, O thou fairest among women, go thy way forth by the footsteps of the flock, and feed thy kids beside the shepherds's tents.

9 I have compared thee, O my love, to a company of horses in Pharaoh's chariots.

10 Thy cheeks are comely with rows *of jewels*, thy neck with chains *of gold*.

11 We will make thee borders of gold with studs of silver.

12 While the king *sitteth* at his table, my spikenard sendeth forth the smell thereof.

13 A bundle of myrrh *is* my well-beloved unto me; he shall lie all night betwixt my breasts.

14 My beloved *is* unto me *as* a cluster of camphire in the vineyards of En-gedi.

15 Behold, thou *art* fair, my love; behold, thou *art* fair; thou *hast* doves' eyes.

16 Behold, thou *art* fair, my beloved, **yea,** pleasant: also our bed *is* green.

17 The beams of our house *are* cedar, *and* our rafters of fir.

CHAP. II.

1 I *am* the rose of Sharon, *and* the lily of the valleys.

2 As the lily among thorns, so *is* my love among the daughters.

3 As the apple-tree among the trees of the wood, so *is* my beloved among the sons. I sat down under his shadow with great delight, and his fruit *was* sweet to my taste.

4 He brought me to the banqueting house, and his banner over me *was* love.

5 Stay me with flagons, comfort me with apples: for I *am* sick of love.

6 His left hand *is* under my head, and his right hand doth embrace me.

7 I charge you, O ye daughters of Jerusalem, by the roes, and by the hinds of the field, that ye stir not up, nor awake *my* love, till he please.

8 The voice of my beloved! behold, he cometh leaping upon the mountains, skipping upon the hills.

9 My beloved is like a roe, or a young hart: behold, he standeth behind our wall, he looketh forth at the windows, shewing himself through the lattice.

10 My beloved spake, and said unto me, Rise up, my love, my fair one, and come away.

11 For lo, the winter is past, the rain is over *and* gone ;

12 The flowers appear on the earth ; the time of the singing *of birds* is come, and the voice of the turtle is heard in our land ;

13 The fig-tree putteth forth her green figs, and the vines *with* the tender grape give a *good* smell. Arise, my love, my fair one, and come away.

14 O my dove, *that art* in the clefts of the rock, in the secret *places* of the stairs, let me see thy countenance, let me hear thy voice; for sweet *is* thy voice, and thy countenance *is* comely.

15 Take us the foxes, the little foxes, that spoil the vines : for our vines *have* tender grapes.

16 My beloved *is* mine, and I *am* his : he feedeth among the lilies.

17 Until the day break, and the shadows flee away, turn, my beloved, and be thou like a roe or a young hart upon the mountains of Bether.

Chap. III.

1 By night on my bed I sought him whom **my** soul loveth: I sought him, but I found him not.

2 I will rise now, and go about the city in the streets, and in the broad ways I will seek him whom my soul loveth: I sought him, but I found him not.

3 The watchmen that go about the city found me: *to whom I said,* Saw ye him whom my soul loveth?

4 *It was* but a little that I passed from them, but I found him whom my soul loveth: I held him, and would not let him go, until I had brought him into my mother's house, and into the chamber of her that conceived me.

5 I charge you, O ye daughters of Jerusalem, by the roes, and by the hinds of the field, that ye stir not up, nor awake *my* love, till he please.

6 What *is* this that cometh out of the wilderness like pillars of smoke, perfumed with myrrh and frankincense, with all powders of the merchant?

7 Behold his bed, which *is* Solomon's: threescore valiant men *are* about it, of the valiant of Israel.

8 They all hold swords, *being* expert in war: every man *hath* his sword upon his thigh because of fear in the night.

9 King Solomon made himself a chariot of the wood of Lebanon.

10 He made the pillars thereof *of* silver, the bottom thereof *of* gold, the covering of it *of* purple, the midst thereof being paved *with* love, for the daughters of Jerusalem.

11 Go forth, O ye daughters of Zion, and behold king Solomon with the crown wherewith his mother crowned him in the day of his espousals, and in the day of the gladness of his heart.

Chap. IV.

1 Behold, thou *art* fair, my love; behold, thou *art* fair; thou *hast* dove's eyes within thy locks: thy hair *is* as a flock of goats, that appear from mount Gilead.

2 Thy teeth *are* like a flock *of sheep that are even* shorn, which came up from the washing; whereof every one bear twins, and none is barren among them.

3 Thy lips *are* like a thread of scarlet, and thy speech *is* comely: thy temples *are* like a piece of a pomegranate within thy locks.

4 Thy neck *is* like the tower of David builded for an armory, whereon there hang a thousand bucklers, all shields of mighty men.

5 Thy two breasts *are* like two young roes that are twins, which feed among the lilies.

6 Until the day break, and the shadows flee away, I will get me to the mountain of myrrh, and to the hill of frankincense.

7 Thou *art* all fair, my love; *there is* no spot in thee.

8 Come with me from Lebanon, *my* spouse, with me from Lebanon: look from the top of Amana, from the top of Shenir and Hermon, from the lions' dens, from the mountains of the leopards.

9 Thou hast ravished my heart, my sister, *my* spouse; thou hast ravished my heart with one of thine eyes, with one chain of thy neck.

10 How fair is thy love, my sister, *my* spouse! how much better is thy love than wine! and the smell of thine ointments than all spices!

11 Thy lips, O *my* spouse, drop *as* the honey-comb: honey and milk *are* under thy tongue; and the smell of thy garments *is* like the smell of Lebanon.

12 A garden inclosed *is* my sister, *my* spouse; a spring shut up, a fountain sealed.

13 Thy plants *are* an orchard of pomegranates, with pleasant fruits; camphire, with spikenard.

14 Spikenard and saffron; calamus and cinnamon, with all trees of frankincense; myrrh and aloes, with all the chief spices:

15 A fountain of gardens, a well of living waters, and streams from Lebanon.

16 Awake, O north wind; and come, thou south, blow upon my garden, *that* the spices thereof may flow out. Let my beloved come into his garden, and eat his pleasant fruits.

CHAP. V.

1 I am come into my garden, my sister, *my* spouse: I have gathered my myrrh with my spice; I have eaten my honey-comb with my honey; I have drunk my wine with my milk: eat, O friends; drink, yea, drink abundantly, O beloved.

2 I sleep, but my heart waketh: *it is* the voice of my beloved that knocketh, *saying*, Open to me, my sister, my love, my dove, my undefiled: for my head is filled with dew, *and* my locks with the drops of the night.

3 I have put off my coat; how shall I put it on? I have washed my feet; how shall I defile them?

4 My beloved put in his hand by the hole *of the door*, and my bowels were moved for him.

5 I rose up to open to my beloved; and my hands dropped *with* myrrh, and my fingers *with* sweet-smelling myrrh, upon the handles of the lock.

6 I opened to my beloved; but my beloved had withdrawn himself, *and* was gone: my soul failed when he spake: I sought him, but I could not find him; I called him, but he gave me no answer.

7 The watchmen that went about the city found me, they smote me, they wounded me: the keepers of the walls took away my vail from me.

8 I charge you, O daughters of Jerusalem, if ye find my beloved, that ye tell him, that I *am* sick of love.

9 What *is* thy beloved more than *another* beloved, O thou fairest among women? what *is* thy beloved more than *another* beloved, that thou dost so charge us?

10 My beloved *is* white and ruddy, the chiefest among ten thousand.

11 His head *is as* the most fine gold, his locks *are* bushy, *and* black as a raven.

12 His eyes *are* as *the eyes* of doves by the rivers of waters, washed with milk, *and* fitly set.

13 His cheeks *are* as a bed of spices, *as* sweet flowers; his lips *like* lilies, dropping sweet-smelling myrrh.

14 His hands *are as* gold rings set with the beryl: his belly *is as* bright ivory overlaid with sapphires.

15 His legs *are as* pillars of marble, set upon sockets of fine gold; his countenance *is* as Lebanon, excellent as the cedars.

16 His mouth *is* most sweet: yea, he *is* altogether lovely. This *is* my beloved, and this *is* my friend, O daughters of Jerusalem.

Chap. VI.

1 Whither is thy beloved gone, O thou fairest among women? whither is thy beloved turned aside? that we may seek him with thee.

2 My beloved is gone down into his garden, to the bed of spices, to feed in the gardens, and to gather lilies.

3 I *am* my beloved's and my beloved *is* mine: he feedeth among the lilies.

4 Thou *art* beautiful, O my love, as Tirzah, comely as Jerusalem, terrible as *an army* with banners.

5 Turn away thine eyes from me, for they have overcome me: thy hair *is* as a flock of goats that appear from Gilead.

6 Thy teeth *are* as a flock of sheep which go up from the washing, whereof every one beareth twins, and *there is* not one barren among them.

7 As a piece of a pomegranate *are* thy temples within thy locks.

8 There are threescore queens, and fourscore concubines, and virgins without number.

9 My dove, my undefiled is *but* one; she *is* the *only* one of her mother, she *is* the choice *one* of her that bare her. The daughters saw her, and blessed her; *yea*, the queens and the concubines, and they praised her.

10 Who *is* she *that* looketh forth as the morning, fair as the moon, clear as the sun, *and* terrible as *an army* with banners?

11 I went down into the garden of nuts to see the fruits of the valley, *and* to see whether the vine flourished, *and* the pomegranates budded.

12 Or ever I was aware, my soul made me *like* the chariots of Ammi-nadib.

13 Return, return, O Shulamite: return, return, that we may look upon thee. What will ye see in the Shulamite? As it were the company of two armies.

CHAP. VII

1 How beautiful are thy feet with shoes, O prince's daughter! the joints of thy thighs *are* like jewels, the work of the hands of a cunning workman.

2 Thy navel *is like* a round goblet, *which* want-

eth not liquor: thy belly *is like* a heap of wheat set about with lilies.

3 Thy two breasts *are* like two young roes *that are* twins.

4 Thy neck *is* as a tower of ivory; thine eyes *like* the fishpools in Heshbon, by the gate of Bath-rabbim: thy nose *is* as the tower of Lebanon which looketh toward Damascus.

5 Thine head upon thee *is* like Carmel, and the hair of thine head like purple; the King *is* held in the galleries.

6 How fair and how pleasant art thou, O love, for delights!

7 This thy stature is like to a palm tree, and thy breasts to clusters *of grapes.*

8 I said, I will go up to the palm tree, I will take hold of the boughs thereof: now also thy breasts shall be as clusters of the vine, and the smell of thy nose like apples:

9 And the roof of thy mouth like the best wine for my beloved, that goeth *down* sweetly, causing the lips of those that are asleep to speak.

10 I *am* my beloved's, and his desire *is* toward me.

11 Come, my beloved, let us go forth into the field; let us lodge in the villages.

12 Let us get up early to the vineyards; let us see if the vine flourish, *whether* the tender grape appear, *and* the pomegranates bud forth: there will I give thee my loves.

13 The mandrakes give a smell, and at our gates *are* all manner of pleasant *fruits,* new and old, *which* I have laid up for thee, O my beloved.

CHAP. VIII.

1 O that thou *wert* as my brother, that sucked the breasts of my mother! *when* I should find thee

without, I would kiss thee; yea, I should not **be** despised.

2 I would lead thee, *and* bring thee into my mother's house, *who* would instruct me: I would cause thee to drink of spiced wine of the juice of my pomegranate.

3 His left hand *should be* under my head, and his right hand should embrace me.

4 I charge you, O daughters of Jerusalem, that ye stir not up, nor awake *my* love, until he please.

5 Who *is* this that cometh up from the wilderness, leaning upon her beloved? I raised thee up under the apple tree: there thy mother brought thee forth; there she brought thee forth *that* bare thee.

6 Set me as a seal upon thine heart, as a seal upon thine arm: for love *is* strong as death: jealousy *is* cruel as the grave: the coals thereof *are* coals of fire, *which hath* a most vehement flame.

7 Many waters cannot quench love, neither can the floods drown it: if a man would give all the substance of his house for love, it would utterly be contemned.

8 We have a little sister, and she hath no breasts: what shall we do for our sister in the day when she shall be spoken for?

9 If she *be* a wall, we will build upon her a palace of silver: and if she *be* a door, we will inclose her with boards of cedar.

10 I *am* a wall, and my breasts like towers: then was I in his eyes as one that found favor.

11 Solomon had a vineyard at Baalhamon; he let out the vineyard unto keepers; every one for the fruit thereof was to bring a thousand *pieces* of silver.

12 My vineyard, which *is* mine, *is* before me: thou, O Solomon, *must have* a thousand, and those that keep the fruit thereof two hundred.

13 Thou that dwellest in the gardens, the companions hearken to thy voice: cause me to hear *it.*

14 Make haste, my beloved, and be thou like to a roe or to a young hart upon the mountains of spices.

ISAIAH.

Chap. I.

21 How is the faithful city become a harlot?

Chap. III.

16 Moreover the Lord saith, Because the daughters of Zion are haughty, and walk with stretched forth necks and wanton eyes, walking and mincing *as* they go, and making a tinkling with their feet:

17 Therefore the Lord will smite with a scab the crown of the head of the daughters of Zion, and the Lord will discover their secret parts.

18 In that day the Lord will take away the bravery of *their* tinkling ornaments *about their feet,* and *their* cauls, and *their* round tires like the moon.

24 And it shall come to pass, *that* instead of sweet smell there shall be stink; and instead of a girdle a rent; and instead of well-set hair baldness.

Chap. IV.

1 And in that day seven women shall take hold of one man, saying, We will eat our own bread, and wear our own apparel: only let us be called by thy name, to take away our reproach.

Chap. VII.

14 Therefore the Lord himself shall give you a sign; Behold, a virgin shall conceive, and bear a son, and shall call his name Immanuel.

Chap. VIII.

3 And I went unto the prophetess; and **she** conceived, and bare a son. Then said the LORD to me, Call his name Maher-shalal-hash-baz.

Chap. IX.

14 Therefore the LORD will cut off from Israel head and tail, branch and rush, in one day.

15 The ancient and honorable, he *is* the head; and the prophet that teacheth lies, he *is* the tail.

Chap. XIII.

16 Their children also shall be dashed to pieces before their eyes; their houses shall be spoiled, and their wives ravished.

Chap. XIX.

14 The LORD hath mingled a perverse spirit in the midst thereof: and they have caused Egypt to err in every work thereof as a drunken *man* staggereth in his vomit.

15 Neither shall there be *any* work for Egypt, which the head or tail, branch or rush, may do.

16 In that day shall Egypt be like unto women.

Chap. XX.

2 At the same time spake the LORD by Isaiah the son of Amoz, saying, Go and loose the sackcloth from off thy loins, and put off thy shoe from thy foot. And he did so, walking naked and barefoot.

3 And the LORD said, Like as my servant Isaiah hath walked naked and barefoot three years *for* a sign and wonder upon Egypt and upon Ethiopia;

4 So shall the king of Assyria lead away the Egyptians prisoners, and the Ethiopians captives, young and old, naked and barefoot, even with *their* buttocks uncovered, to the shame of Egypt.

Chap. XXI.

3 Therefore are my loins filled with pain : pangs nave taken hold upon me, as the pangs of a woman that travaileth : I was bowed down at the hearing *of it.*

Chap. XXVI.

17 Like as a woman with child, *that* draweth near the time of her delivery, is in pain, *and* crieth out in her pangs; so have we been in thy sight, O Lord.

18 We have been with child, we have been in pain, we have as it were brought forth wind; we have not wrought any deliverance in the earth.

Chap. XXVIII.

7 The priest and the prophet have erred through strong drink, they are swallowed up of wine, they are out of the way through strong drink; they err in vision, they stumble *in* judgment.

8 For all tables are full of vomit *and* filthiness, *so that there is* no place *clean.*

9 Whom shall he teach knowledge ? and whom shall he make to understand doctrine? *them that are* weaned from the milk, *and* drawn from the breasts.

Chap. XXXII.

11 Tremble, ye women that are at ease; be troubled, ye careless ones : strip you, and make you bare, and gird *sackcloth* upon your *loins.*

12 They shall lament for the teats, for the pleasant fields, for the fruitful vine.

Chap. XXXVII.

36 Then the angel of the Lord went forth, and smote in the camp of the Assyrians a hundred and fourscore and five thousand : and when they arose early in the morning, behold, they *were* all dead corpses.

Chap. XXXIX.

7 And of thy sons that shall issue from thee, which thou shalt beget, shall they take away ; and they shall be eunuchs in the palace of the king of Babylon.

Chap. XLII.

13 The LORD shall go forth as a mighty man, he shall stir up jealousy like a man of war : he shall cry, yea, roar; he shall prevail against his enemies.

14 I have long time holden my peace; I have been still, *and* refrained myself : *now* will I cry like a travailing woman : I will destroy and devour at once.

Chap. XLIV.

2 Thus saith the LORD that made thee, and formed thee from the womb.

Chap. XLV.

10 Woe unto him that saith unto *his* father, What begettest thou? or to the woman, What hast thou brought forth?

Chap. XLVII.

1 Come down, and sit in the dust, O virgin daughter of Babylon, sit on the ground : *there is* no throne, O daughter of the Chaldeans : for thou shalt no more be called tender and delicate.

2 Take the millstones, and grind meal : uncover thy locks, make bare the leg, uncover the thigh, pass over the rivers.

3 Thy nakedness shall be uncovered, yea, thy name shall be seen : I will take vengeance, and I will not meet *thee as* a man.

Chap. XLVIII.

8 I knew that thou wouldest deal very treacher-ously, and wast called a transgressor from the **womb**

19 Thy seed also had been as the sand, and the offspring of thy bowels like the gravel thereof.

Chap. XLIX.

15 Can a woman forget her sucking child, that she should not have compassion on the son of her womb? yea, they may forget, yet will I not forget thee.

Chap. LIV.

1 Sing, O barren, thou *that* didst not bear; break forth into singing, and cry aloud, thou *that* didst not travail with child : for more *are* the children of the desolate than the children of the married wife, saith the LORD.

Chap. LVI.

3 Neither let the eunuchs say, Behold, I *am* a dry tree.

Chap. LVII.

3 But draw near hither, ye sons of the sorceress, the seed of the adulterer and the whore.

4 Against whom do ye sport yourselves? against whom make ye a wide mouth, *and* draw out the tongue? *are* ye not children of transgression, a seed of falsehood;

5 Inflaming yourselves with idols under every green tree?

7 Upon a lofty and high mountain hast thou set thy bed: even thither wentest thou up to offer sacrifice.

8 Behind the doors also and the posts hast thou set up thy remembrance : for thou hast discovered *thyself to another* than me, and art gone up; thou hast enlarged thy bed, and made thee *a covenant* with them; thou lovedst their bed where thou sawest *it.*

Chap. LX.

16 Thou shalt also suck the milk of the Gen-tiles, and shall suck the breast of kings.

Chap. LXIV.

6 But we are all as an unclean *thing*, and **all our** righteousnesses *are* as filthy rags.

Chap. LXVI.

7 Before she travailed, she brought forth; before her pain came, she was delivered of a manchild.

8 Who hath heard such a thing? who hath seen such things? shall the earth be made to bring forth in one day? *or* shall a nation be born at once? for as soon as Zion travailed, she brought forth her children.

9 Shall I bring to the birth, and not cause to bring forth? saith the LORD: shall I cause to bring forth, and shut *the womb?* saith thy God.

11 That ye may suck, and be satisfied with the breasts of her consolations; that ye may milk out, and be delighted with the abundance of her glory.

JEREMIAH.

Chap. I.

5 Before I formed thee in the belly, I knew thee; and before thou camest forth out of the womb I sanctified thee, *and* I ordained thee a prophet unto the nations.

Chap. II.

20 Upon every high hill and under every green tree thou wanderest, playing the harlot.

22 For though thou wash thee with nitre, and take thee much soap, *yet* thine iniquity is marked before me, saith the Lord GOD.

33 Why trimmest thou thy way to seek love?

34 Also in thy skirts is found the blood of the souls of the poor innocents.

36 Why gaddest thou about so much to change thy way?

Chap. III.

1 They say, if a man put away his wife, and she go from him, and become another man's, shall he return unto her again? shall not that land be greatly polluted? but thou hast played the harlot with many lovers; yet return again to me, saith the LORD.

2 Lift up thine eyes unto the high places, and see where thou hast not been lain with. In the ways hast thou sat for them, as the Arabian in the wilderness; and thou hast polluted the land with thy whoredoms, and with thy wickedness.

3 Thou hadst a whore's forehead, thou refusedst to be ashamed.

6 The LORD said also unto me in the days of Josiah the king, Hast thou seen *that* which backsliding Israel hath done? she is gone up upon every high mountain, and under every green tree, and there hath played the harlot.

7 And I said after she had done all these *things*, Turn thou unto me. But she returned not. And her treacherous sister Judah saw *it.*

8 And I saw, when for all the causes whereby backsliding Israel committed adultery, I had put her away, and given her a bill of divorce; yet her treacherous sister Judah feared not, but went and played the harlot also.

9 And it came to pass through the lightness of her whoredom, that she defiled the land, and committed adultery with stones and with stocks.

10 And yet for all this, her treacherous sister Judah hath not turned unto me with her whole heart, but feignedly, saith the LORD.

Chap. IV.

19 My bowels, my bowels! I am pained at my very heart; my heart maketh a noise in me: I cannot hold my peace.

31 For I have heard a voice as of a woman in travail, *and* the anguish as of her that bringeth forth her first child.

Chap. V.

7 When I had fed them to the full, they then committed adultery, and assembled themselves by troops in the harlots' houses.

8 They were *as* fed horses in the morning: every one neighed after his neighbor's wife.

Chap. XIII.

21 What wilt thou say when he shall punish thee? for thou hast taught them *to be* captains, *and* as chief over thee: shall not sorrows take thee, as a woman in travail?

22 For the greatness of thine iniquity are thy skirts discovered, *and* thy heels made bare.

26 Therefore will I discover thy skirts upon thy face, that thy shame may appear.

27 I have seen thine adulteries, and thy neighings, the lewdness of thy whoredom, *and* thine abominations on the hills in the fields.

Chap. XIV.

5 Yea, the hind also calved in the field, and forsook *it*, because there was no grass.

Chap. XVI.

4 They shall die of grievous deaths; they shall not be lamented; neither shall they be buried; *but* they shall be as dung upon the face of the earth.

Chap. XX.

14 Cursed *be* the day wherein I was born; let

not the day wherein my mother bare me be blessed.

15 Cursed *be* the man who brought tidings to my father, saying, A man-child is born unto thee ; making him very glad.

17 Because he slew me not from the womb; or that my mother might have been my grave, and her womb *to be* always great *with me.*

18 Wherefore came I forth out of the womb to see labor and sorrow, that my days should be consumed with shame ?

Chap. XXII.

23 O inhabitant of Lebanon, that makest thy nest in the cedars, how gracious shalt thou be when pangs come upon thee, the pain as of a woman in travail !

24 *As* I live, saith the Lord.

26 I will cast thee out, and thy mother that bare thee, into another country, where ye were not born ; and there shall ye die.

Chap. XXIII.

23 For the land is full of adulterers.

Chap. XXV.

27 Therefore thou shalt say unto them, Thus saith the Lord of hosts, the God of Israel ; Drink ye, and be drunken, and spew, and fall, and rise no more, because of the sword which I will send among you.

28 And it shall be, if they refuse to take the cup at thy hand to drink, then shalt thou say unto them, Thus saith the Lord of hosts; Ye shall certainly drink.

33 And the slain of the Lord shall be at that day from *one* end of the earth even unto the *other* end of the earth : they shall not be lamented, neither gathered, nor buried; they shall be dung upon the ground.

Chap. XXX.

1 The word that came to Jeremiah from **the** LORD, saying,

5 For thus saith the LORD;

6 Ask ye now, and see whether a man doth travail with child? wherefore do I see every man with his hands on his loins as a woman in travail.

Chap. XXXI.

8 The woman with child in her that travaileth with child together: a great company shall return thither.

21 O virgin of Israel, turn again to these thy cities.

22 How long wilt thou go about, O thou back-sliding daughter? for the LORD hath created a new thing in the earth. A woman shall compass a man.

27 Behold, the days come, saith the LORD, that I will sow the house of Israel and the house of Judah with the seed of man, and with the seed of beast.

Chap. XXXVIII.

6 And they let down Jeremiah with cords. And in the dungeon *there was* no water, but mire: so Jeremiah sunk in the mire.

7 Now when Ebed-melech the Ethiopian, one of the eunuchs which was in the king's house, heard that they had put Jeremiah in the dungeon;

11 Ebed-melech took the men with him, and went into the house of the king under the treasury, and took thence old cast clouts and old rotten rags, and let them down by cords into the dungeon to Jeremiah.

12 And Ebed-melech the Ethiopian said unto Jeremiah, Put now *these* old cast clouts and rotten

rags under thine arm-holes under the cords. And Jeremiah did so.

13 So they drew up Jeremiah with cords, and took him up out of the dungeon: and Jeremiah remained in the court of the prison.

CHAP. XLVI.

20 Egypt *is like* a very fair heifer, *but* destruction cometh.

21 Also her hired men *are* in the midst of her like fatted bullocks.

CHAP. XLVIII.

26 Make ye him drunken; for he magnified *himself* against the LORD: Moab also shall wallow in his vomit, and he also shall be in derision.

41 And the mighty men's hearts in Moab at that day shall be as the heart of a woman in her pangs.

CHAP XLIX.

10 But I have made Esau bare, I have uncovered his secret places, and he shall not be able to hide himself: his seed is spoiled, and his brethren, and his neighbors, and he *is* not.

22 And at that day shall the heart of the mighty men of Edom be as the heart of a woman in her pangs.

24 Damascus is waxed feeble, *and* turneth herself to flee, and fear hath seized on *her:* anguish and sorrows have taken her, as a woman in travail.

CHAP. L.

11 O ye destroyers of mine heritage, because ye are grown fat as the heifer at grass, and bellow as bulls;

12 Your mother shall be sore confounded; she that bare you shall be ashamed: behold, the hindermost of the nations *shall be* a wilderness.

43 The king of Babylon hath heard the report

of them, and his hands waxed feeble: anguish took hold of him, *and* pangs as of a woman in travail.

CHAP. LI.

40 I will bring them down like lambs to the slaughter, like rams with he-goats.

THE LAMENTATIONS OF JEREMIAH.

CHAP. I.

8 Jerusalem hath grievously sinned; therefore she is removed: all that honored her despise her, because they have seen her nakedness: yea, she sigheth, and turneth backward.

9 Her filthiness *is* in her skirts.

15 The LORD hath trodden the virgin, the daughter of Judah, *as* in a wine-press.

19 I called for my lovers, *but* they deceived me: my priests and mine elders gave up the ghost in the city.

20 Behold, O LORD; for I *am* in distress: my bowels are troubled; mine heart is turned within me.

CHAP. II.

20 Behold, O LORD, and consider to whom thou hast done this. Shall the women eat their fruit, *and* children of a span long?

CHAP. IV.

5 They that did feed delicately are desolate in the streets: they that were brought up in scarlet embrace dunghills.

21 Rejoice and be glad, O daughters of Edom; . . the cup also shall pass through unto thee:

thou shalt be drunken, and shalt make thyself
naked.

CHAP. V.

11 They ravished the women in Zion, *and* the
maids in the cities of Judah.

EZEKIEL.

CHAP. IV.

10 And thy meat which thou shalt eat *shall be*
by weight, twenty shekels a day: from time to
time shalt thcu eat it.

12 And thou shalt eat it *as* barley cakes, and
thou shalt bake it with dung that cometh out of
man, in their sight.

13 And the LORD said, Even thus shall the
children of Israel eat their defiled bread among
the Gentiles, whither I will drive them.

14 Then said I, Ah Lord God! behold, my soul
hath not been polluted: for from my youth up
even till now have I not eaten of that which dieth
of itself, or is torn in pieces; neither came there
abominable flesh into my mouth.

15 Then he said unto me, Lo, I have given thee
cow's dung for man's dung, and thou shalt prepare
thy bread therewith.

CHAP. XVI.

3 Thus saith the Lord God unto Jerusalem,
Thy birth and thy nativity *is* of the land of Canaan.

4 And *as for* thy nativity, in the day thou wast
born thy navel was not cut, neither wast thou
washed in water to supple *thee;* thou wast not
salted at all, nor swaddled at all.

5 Thou wast cast out in the open field, to the

loathing of thy person, in the day that thou **wast** born.

6 I said unto thee *when thou wast* in thy blood, Live.

7 *Thy* breasts are fashioned, and thine hair is grown, whereas thou *wast* naked and bare.

8 Now when I passed by thee, and looked upon thee, behold, thy time *was* the time of love; and I spread my skirt over thee, and covered thy nakedness: yea, I sware unto thee, and entered into a covenant with thee, saith the Lord God, and thou becamest mine.

9 Then washed I thee with water; yea, I thoroughly washed away thy blood from thee, and I anointed thee with oil.

10 I clothed thee also with broidered work, and shod thee with badger's skin, and I girded thee about with fine linen, and I covered thee with silk

11 I decked thee also with ornaments, and I put bracelets upon thine hands, and a chain on thy neck.

12 And I put a jewel on thy forehead, and earrings in thine ears, and a beautiful crown upon thine head.

13 Thus wast thou decked with gold and silver, and thy raiment *was of* fine linen, and silk, and broidered work; thou didst eat fine flour, and honey, and oil; and thou wast exceeding beautiful, and thou didst prosper into a kingdom.

14 And thy renown went forth among the heathen for thy beauty: for it *was* perfect through my comeliness, which I had put upon thee, saith the Lord God.

15 But thou didst trust in thine own beauty, and playedst the harlot because of thy renown, and pouredst out thy fornications on every one **that** passed by; his it was.

20 Moreover, thou hast taken thy sons and thy

daughters, whom thou hast borne unto me, and these hast thou sacrificed unto them to be devoured. *Is this* of thy whoredoms a small matter?

22 And in all thine abominations and thy whoredoms thou hast not remembered the days of thy youth, when thou wast naked and bare, *and* wast polluted in thy blood.

25 Thou hast built thy high place at every head of the way, and hast made thy beauty to be abhorred, and hast opened thy feet to every one that passed by, and multiplied thy whoredoms.

26 Thou hast also committed fornication with the Egyptians thy neighbors, great of flesh; and hast increased thy whoredoms, to provoke me to anger.

27 Behold, therefore I have stretched out my hand over thee, and have diminished thine ordinary *food*, and delivered thee unto the will of them that hate thee, the daughters of the Philistines, which are ashamed of thy lewd way.

28 Thou hast played the whore also with the Assyrians, because thou wast unsatiable; yea, thou hast played the harlot with them, and yet couldest not be satisfied.

29 Thou hast, moreover, multiplied thy fornication in the land of Canaan unto Chaldea; and yet thou wast not satisfied herewith.

30 How weak is thine heart, saith the Lord GOD, seeing thou dost all these *things*, the work of an imperious, whorish woman,

31 In that thou buildest thine eminent place in the head of every way, and makest thine high place in every street; and hast not been as a harlot, in that thou scornest **hire**;

32 *But as* a wife that committeth adultery, *which* taketh strangers instead of her husband!

33 They give gifts to all whores: but thou givest thy gifts to all thy lovers, and hirest them,

that they may come unto thee on every side for
thy whoredom.

34 And the contrary is in thee from *other* women
in thy whoredoms, whereas none followeth thee to
commit whoredoms : and in that thou givest a
reward, and no reward is given unto thee ; therefore thou art contrary.

35 Wherefore, O harlot, hear the word of the
LORD :

36 Thus saith the Lord God ; Because thy filthiness was poured out, and thy nakedness discovered through thy whoredoms with thy lovers, and
with all the idols of thy abominations, and by the
blood of thy children, which thou didst give unto
them ;

37 Behold, therefore, I will gather all thy lovers,
with whom thou hast taken pleasure, and all *them*
that thou hast loved, with all *them* that thou hast
hated ; I will even gather them round about against
thee, and will discover thy nakedness unto them,
that they may see all thy nakedness.

38 And I will judge thee, as women that break
wedlock and shed blood are judged; and I will
give thee blood in fury and jealousy.

39 And I will also give thee into their hand,
and they shall throw down thine eminent place,
and shall break down thy high places : they shall
strip thee also of thy clothes, and shall take thy
fair jewels, and leave thee naked and bare.

41 And I will cause thee to cease from playing
the harlot, and thou also shalt give no hire any
more.

42 So will I make my fury toward thee to rest,
and my jealousy shall depart from thee, and I will
be quiet, and will be no more angry.

43 Because thou hast not remembered the days
of thy youth, but hast fretted me in all these *things;*

behold, therefore, I also will recompense thy way upon *thine* head, saith the Lord GOD : and thou shalt not commit this lewdness above all thine abominations,

CHAP. XVIII.

5 But if a man be just, and do that which is lawful and right,

6 Neither hath defiled his neighbor's wife, neither hath come near to a menstruous woman,

9 He *is* just, he shall surely live, saith the Lord GOD.

10 If he beget a son *that is* a robber, a shedder of blood,

14 Now lo, *if* he beget a son that seeth all his father's sins which he hath done, and considereth, and doeth not such like.

CHAP. XIX.

1 Moreover, take thou up a lamentation for the princes of Israel,

2 And say, What *is* thy mother? A lioness : she lay down among lions, she nourished her whelps among the lions.

3 And she brought up one of her whelps : it became a young lion, and it learned to catch the prey ; it devoured men.

CHAP. XXII.

3 Then say thou, Thus saith the Lord GOD ; The city sheddeth blood in the midst of it.

9 In thee are men that carry tales to shed blood : and in thee they eat upon the mountains : in the midst of thee they commit lewdness.

10 In thee have they discovered their fathers' nakedness : in thee have they humbled her that was set apart for pollution.

11 And one hath committed abomination with his neighbor's wife ; and another hath lewdly de-

filed his daughter in law ; and another in thee hath humbled his sister, his father's daughter.

28 And her prophets have daubed them with untempered *mortar*, seeing vanity, and divining lies unto them, saying, Thus saith the Lord GOD, when the LORD hath not spoken.

CHAP. XXIII.

1 The word of the LORD came again unto me, saying,

2 Son of man, there were two women, the daughters of one mother:

3 And they committed whoredoms in Egypt; they committed whoredom in their youth: there were their breasts pressed, and there they bruised the teats of their virginity.

4 And the names of them *were* Aholah the elder, and Aholibah her sister: and they were mine, and they bare sons and daughters. Thus *were* their names; Samaria *is* Aholah, and Jerusalem Aholibah.

5 And Aholah played the harlot when she was mine; and she doted on her lovers, on the Assyrians *her* neighbors.

6 *Which were* clothed with blue, captains and rulers, all of them desirable young men.

7 Thus she committed her whoredoms with them, with all them *that were* the chosen men of Assyria, and with all on whom she doted; with all their idols she defiled herself.

8 Neither left she her whoredoms *brought* from Egypt: for in her youth they lay with her, and they bruised the breasts of her virginity, and poured their whoredom upon her.

9 Wherefore I have delivered her into the hand of her lovers, into the hand of the Assyrians, upon whom she doted.

10 These discovered her nakedness; they took her sons and her daughters, and slew her with the sword : and she became famous among women ; for they had executed judgment upon her.

11 And when her sister Aholibah saw *this*, she was more corrupt in her inordinate love than she, and in her whoredoms more than her sister in *her* whoredoms.

12 She doted upon the Assyrians *her* neighbors, captains and rulers clothed most gorgeously, horsemen riding upon horses, all of them desirable young men.

13 Then I saw that she was defiled, *that* they *took* both one way ;

14 And *that* she increased her whoredoms : for when she saw men portrayed upon the wall, the images of the Chaldeans portrayed with vermilion,

15 Girded with girdles upon their loins, exceeding in dyed attire upon their heads, all of them princes to look to, after the manner of the Babylonians of Chaldea, the land of their nativity :

16 And as soon as she saw them with her eyes, she doted upon them, and sent messengers unto them into Chaldea.

17 And the Babylonians came to her in the bed of love, and they defiled her with their whoredom, and she was polluted with them, and her mind was alienated from them.

18 So she discovered her whoredoms, and discovered her nakedness : then my mind was alienated from her as my mind was alienated from her sister.

19 Yet she multiplied her whoredoms, in calling to remembrance the days of her youth, wherein she had played the harlot in the land of Egypt.

20 For she doted upon their paramours, whose flesh *is as* the flesh of asses, and whose issue *is like* the issue of horses.

21 Thus thou calledst to remembrance the lewdness of thy youth, in bruising thy teats by the Egyptians for the paps of thy youth.

25 And I will set my jealousy against thee, and they shall deal furiously with thee : they shall take away thy nose and thine ears.

26 They shall also strip thee out of thy clothes, and take away thy fair jewels.

27 Thus will I make thy lewdness to cease from thee, and thy whoredom *brought* from the land of Egypt:

29 And they shall deal with thee hatefully, and shall take away all thy labor, and shall leave thee naked and bare : and the nakedness of thy whoredoms shall be discovered, both thy lewdness and thy whoredoms.

30 I will do these *things* unto thee, because thou hast gone a whoring after the heathen.

34 Thou shalt even drink it and suck *it* out, and thou shalt break the sherds thereof, and pluck off thine own breasts : for I have spoken *it*, saith the Lord GOD.

43 Then said I unto *her that was* old in adulteries, Will they now commit whoredoms with her, and she *with them?*

44 Yet they went in unto her, as they go in unto a woman that playeth the harlot: so went they in unto Aholah and unto Aholibah, the lewd woman.

CHAP. XXIX.

4 But I will put hooks in thy jaws, and I will cause the fish of thy rivers to stick unto thy scales, and I will bring thee up out of the midst of thy rivers, and all the fish of thy rivers shall stick unto thy scales.

CHAP. XXXIX.

11 And it shall come to pass in that day, *that*

I will give unto Gog a place there of graves in Israel, the valley of the passengers on the east of the sea: and it shall stop the *noses* of the passengers: and there shall they bury Gog and all his multitude: and they shall call *it* The valley of Hamon-gog.

———

HOSEA.

Chap. I.

2 And the LORD said to Hosea, Go, take unto thee a wife of whoredoms and children of whoredoms; for the land hath committed great whoredom, *departing* from the LORD.

3 So he went and took Gomer the daughter of Diblaim; which conceived and bare him a son.

6 And she conceived again, and bare a daughter. And *God* said unto him, Call her name Lo-ruhamah.

8 Now when she had weaned Lo-ruhamah, she conceived, and bare a son.

9 Then said *God*, Call his name Lo-ammi: for ye *are* not my people, and I will not be your *God.*

Chap. II.

2 Plead with your mother, plead; for she *is* not my wife, neither *am* I her husband: let her therefore put away her whoredoms out of her sight, and her adulteries from between her breasts;

3 Lest I strip her naked, and set her as in the day that she was born, and make her as a wilderness, and set her like a dry land, and slay her with thirst.

4 And I will not have mercy upon her children; for they *be* the children of whoredoms.

5 For their mother hath played the harlot: she that conceived them hath done shamefully: for she said, I will go after my lovers, that give *me* my bread and my water, my wool and my flax, mine oil and my drink.

7 And she shall follow after her lovers, but she shall not overtake them; and she shall seek them, but shall not find *them:* then shall she say, I will go and return to my first husband; for then *was it* better with me than now.

9 And will recover my wool and my flax *given* to cover her nakedness.

10 And now will I discover her lewdness in the sight of her lovers, and none shall deliver her out of mine hand.

14 Therefore, behold, I will allure her, and bring her into the wilderness, and speak comfortably unto her.

Chap. III.

1 Then said the Lord unto me, Go yet, love a woman beloved of *her* friend, yet an adulteress, according to the love of the Lord toward the children of Israel, who look to other gods, and love flagons of wine.

2 So I bought her to me for fifteen *pieces* of silver, and *for* a homer of barley, and a half homer of barley:

3 And I said unto her, Thou shalt abide for me many days; thou shalt not play the harlot, and thou shalt not be for *another* man: so *will* I also *be* for thee.

Chap. IV.

10 For they shall eat, and not have enough: they shall commit whoredom, and shall not increase.

11 Whoredom and wine and new wine take away the heart.

13 Therefore your daughters shall commit whoredom, and your spouses shall commit adultery.

14 I will not punish your daughters when they commit whoredom, nor your spouses when they commit adultery: for themselves are separated with whores, and they sacrifice with harlots:

15 Though thou, Israel, play the harlot, *yet* let not Judah offend.

16 For Israel slideth back as a back-sliding heifer.

CHAP. V.

12 Therefore *will* I *be* unto Ephraim as a moth, and to the house of Judah as rottenness.

13 When Ephraim saw his sickness, and Judah *saw* his wound, then went Ephraim to the Assyrian, and sent to king Jareb: yet could he not heal you, nor cure you of your wound.

CHAP. VI.

9 And as troops of robbers wait for a man, *so* the company of priests murder in the way by consent: for they commit lewdness.

10 I have seen a horrible thing in the house of Israel: there *is* the whoredom of Ephraim, Israel is defiled.

CHAP. VII.

4 They *are* all adulterers, as an oven heated by the baker, *who* ceaseth from raising after he hath kneaded the dough, until it be leavened.

7 They are all hot as an oven.

8 Ephraim is a cake not turned.

CHAP. IX.

11 *As for* Ephraim, their glory shall fly away like a bird from the birth, and from the womb, and from the conception.

13 Ephraim shall bring forth his children to the murderer.

14 Give them, O Lord: what wilt thou **give?** give them a miscarrying womb and dry breasts.

16 Ephraim is smitten, their root is dried up, they shall bear no fruit: yea, though they bring forth, yet will I slay *even* the beloved *fruit* of their womb.

Chap. X.

10 *It is* in my desire that I should chastise them ;

11 And Ephraim *is as* an heifer *that is* taught, *and* loveth to tread out the *corn;* but I passed over upon her fair neck : I will make Ephraim to ride ; Judah shall plough.

Chap. XII.

3 He [Jacob] took his brother by the heel in the womb.

Chap. XIII.

7 Therefore I will be unto them as a lion : as a leopard by the way will I observe *them.*

8 I will meet them as a bear *that is* bereaved *of her whelps,* and will rend the caul of their heart, and there will I devour them like a lion.

13 The sorrows of a travailing woman shall come upon him : he *is* an unwise son ; for he should not stay long in *the place of* the breaking forth of children.

16 Their infants shall be dashed in pieces, and their women with child shall be ripped up.

JOEL

Chap. III.

3 And they have cast lots for my people, and have given a boy for a harlot, and sold a girl for wine, that they might drink.

AMOS.

Chap. III.

12 Thus saith the Lord: As the shepherd taketh out of the mouth of the lion two legs, or a piece of an ear: so shall the children of Israel be taken out that dwell in Samaria in the corner of a bed, and in Damascus *in* a couch.

Chap. V.

21 I hate, I despise your feast-days, and I will not smell in your solemn assemblies.

Chap. VII.

17 Therefore thus saith the Lord; Thy wife shall he an harlot in the city, and thy sons and thy daughters shall fall by the sword.

JONAH.

Chap. I.

17 Now the Lord had prepared a great fish to swallow up Jonah. And Jonah was in the belly of the fish three days and three nights.

Chap. II.

1 Then Jonah prayed unto the Lord his God out of the fish's belly,

2 And said, I cried by reason of mine affliction unto the Lord, and he heard me; out of the belly of hell cried I, *and* thou heardest my voice.

10 And the Lord spake unto the fish, and it vomited out Jonah upon the dry *land.*

MICAH.

Chap. I.

7 For she gathered *it* of the hire of a harlot, and they shall return to the hire of a harlot.

8 Therefore, I will wail and howl; I will go stripped and naked : I will make a wailing like the dragons, and mourning as the owls.

16 Make thee bald, and poll thee for thy delicate children; enlarge thy baldness as the eagle; for they are gone into captivity from thee.

Chap. II.

1 Woe to them that devise iniquity, and work evil upon their beds! when the morning is light, they practice it, because it is in the power of their hand.

Chap. IV.

9 Now, why dost thou cry out aloud? *is there* no king in thee? is thy counsellor perished? for pangs have taken thee as a woman in travail.

10 Be in pain, and labor to bring forth, O daughter of Zion, like a woman in travail :

11 Many nations are gathered against thee, that say, Let her be defiled.

Chap. VI.

7 Will the Lord be pleased with thousands of rams, *or* with ten thousands of rivers of oil? shall I give my first-born *for* my transgression, the fruit of my body *for* the sin of my soul?

NAHUM.

Chap. III.

3 They stumble upon their corpses :

4 Because of the multitude of the whoredoms

of the well-favored harlot, the mistress of witch crafts, that selleth nations through her whoredoms, and families through her witchcrafts.

5 Behold, I *am* against thee, saith the LORD of hosts; and I will discover thy skirts upon thy face, and I will shew the nations thy nakedness, and the kingdoms thy shame.

6 And I will cast abominable filth upon thee, and make thee vile, and will set thee as a gazing-stock.

HABAKUK.

Chap. II.

15 Woe unto him that giveth his neighbor drink, that puttest thy bottle to *him*, and makest *him* drunken also, that thou mayest look on their nakedness!

16 Thou art filled with shame for glory: drink thou also, and let thy foreskin be uncovered: the cup of the LORD's right hand shall be turned unto thee, and shameful spewing *shall be* on thy glory.

ZECHARIAH.

Chap. IX.

6 And a bastard shall dwell in Ashdod.

Chap. X.

8 I will hiss for them, and gather them.

MALACHI.

Chap. II.

1 And now, O ye priests. this commandment *is* for you.

3 Behold, I will corrupt your seed, and spread dung upon your faces, *even* the dung of your solemn feasts; and *one* shall take you away with it.

11 For Judah hath profaned the holiness of the LORD which he loved, and hath married the daughter of a strange god.

14 Yet ye say, Wherefore? Because the LORD hath been witness between thee and the wife of thy youth, against whom thou hast dealt treacherously: yet *is* she thy companion, and the wife **of thy** covenant.

THE END OF THE OLD TESTAMENT.

THE

NEW TESTAMENT

OF OUR

LORD AND SAVIOUR JESUS CHRIST,

[ABRIDGED]

COMPILED FROM

KING JAMES' TRANSLATION;

AND WITH ALL

STANDARD BIBLES DILIGENTLY COMPARED
AND REVISED.

———

NEW YORK :
INDEPENDENT BIBLE SOCIETY,
INSTITUTED IN THE YEAR MDCCCLXVII.

CHAP. I.

18 Now the birth of Jesus Christ was on this wise: When as his mother Mary was espoused to Joseph, before they came together, she was found with child of the Holy Ghost.

19 Then Joseph her husband, being a just *man*, and not willing to make her a public example, .was minded to put her away privily.

20 But while he thought on these things, behold, the angel of the Lord appeared unto him in a dream, saying, Joseph, thou son of David, fear not to take unto thee Mary thy wife: for that which is conceived in her is of the Holy Ghost.

21 And she shall bring forth a son, and thou shalt call his name JESUS: for he shall save his people from their sins.

22 Now all this was done, that it might be fulfilled which was spoken of the Lord by the prophet, saying,

23 Behold, a virgin shall be with child, and shall bring forth a son, and they shall call his name Emmanuel, which being interpreted is, God with us.

24 Then Joseph, being raised from sleep, did as the angel of the Lord had bidden him, and took unto him his wife:

25 And knew her not till she had brought forth her first-born son: and he called his name JESUS.

CHAP. XIX.

9 And I say unto you, Whosoever shall put away his wife, except *it be* for fornication, and shall marry another, committeth adultery: and whoso marrieth her which is put away, doth commit adultery.

10 His disciples say unto him, If the case of the man be so with *his* wife, it is not good to marry.

12 For there are some eunuchs, which were so born from *their* mother's womb: and there are some eunuchs, which were made eunuchs of men: and there be eunuchs, which have made themselves eunuchs for the kingdom of heaven's sake.

CHAP. XXIV.

19 And woe unto them that are with child, and to them that give suck in those days!

THE GOSPEL ACCORDING TO
ST. MARK.

CHAP. VII.

15 There is nothing from without a man, that entering into him can defile him: but the things which come out of him, those are they that defile the man.

19 Because it entereth not into his heart, but into the belly, and goeth out into the draught, purging all meats?

20 And he said, That which cometh out of the man, that defileth the man.

CHAP. X.

11 And he saith unto them, Whosoever shall put away his wife, and marry another, committeth adultery against her.

12 And if a woman shall put away her husband, and be married to another, she committeth adultery.

CHAP. XIII.

17 But woe to them that are with child, and to them that give suck in those days!

THE GOSPEL ACCORDING TO

ST. LUKE.

CHAP. I.

5 There was in the days of Herod, the king of Judea, a certain priest named Zacharias, of the course of Abia : and his wife *was* of the daughters of Aaron, and her name *was* Elisabeth.

7 And they had no child, because that Elisabeth was barren ; and they both were *now* well stricken in years.

13 But the angel said unto him, Fear not, Zacharias : for thy prayer is heard ; and thy wife Elisabeth shall bare thee a son, and thou shalt call his name John.

15 For he shall be great in the sight of the LORD, and shall drink neither wine nor strong drink ; and he shall be filled with the Holy Ghost, even from his mother's womb.

18 And Zacharias said unto the angel, Whereby

shall I know this? for I am an old man, and my wife well stricken in years.

19 And the angel answering said unto him, I am Gabriel, that stand in the presence of God; and am sent to speak unto thee, and to show thee these glad tidings.

24 And after those days his wife Elisabeth conceived, and hid herself five months, saying,

25 Thus hath the Lord dealt with me in the days wherein he looked on *me*, to take away my reproach among men.

26 And in the sixth month the angel Gabriel was sent from God unto a city of Galilee, named Nazareth,

27 To a virgin espoused to a man whose name was Joseph, of the house of David; and the virgin's name *was* Mary.

28 And the angel came in unto her, and said, Hail, *thou that art* highly favored, the Lord *is* with thee : blessed *art* thou among women.

29 And when she saw *him*, she was troubled at his saying, and cast in her mind what manner of salutation this should be.

30 And the angel said unto her, Fear not, Mary : for thou hast found favor with God.

31 And behold, thou shalt conceive in thy womb, and bring forth a son, and shalt call his name JESUS.

34 Then said Mary unto the angel, How shall this be, seeing I know not a man?

35 And the angel answered and said unto her, The Holy Ghost shall come upon thee, and the power of the Highest shall overshadow thee : therefore also that holy thing which shall be born of thee shall be called the Son of God.

36 And behold, thy cousin Elisabeth, she hath also conceived a son in her old age; and this is the

sixth month with her who was called barren:

37 For with God nothing shall be impossible.

38 And Mary said, Behold the handmaid of the Lord; be it unto me according to thy word. And the angel departed from her.

39 And Mary arose in those days, and went into the hill-country with haste, into a city of Juda;

40 And entered into the house of Zacharias, and saluted Elisabeth.

41 And it came to pass, that when Elisabeth heard the salutation of Mary, the babe leaped in her womb: and Elisabeth was filled with the Holy Ghost.

42 And she spake out with a loud voice and said, Blessed *art* thou among women, and blessed *is* the fruit of thy womb.

43 And whence *is* this to me, that the mother of my Lord should come to me?

44 For lo, as soon as the voice of thy salutation sounded in mine ears, the babe leaped in my womb for joy.

56 And Mary abode with her about three months, and returned to her own house.

57 Now Elisabeth's full time came that she should be delivered: and she brought forth a son.

58 And her neighbors and her cousins heard how the Lord had shewed great mercy upon her; and they rejoiced with her.

59 And it came to pass, that on the eighth day they came to circumcise the child; and they called him Zacharias, after the name of his father.

CHAP. II.

4 And Joseph also went up from Galilee

5 To be taxed with Mary his espoused wife, being great with child.

6 And so it was, that while they were there, the days were accomplished that she should be delivered.

7 And she brought forth her first-born son, and wrapped him in swaddling-clothes, and laid him in a manger.

21 And when eight days were accomplished for the circumcising of the child, his name was called JESUS, which was so named of the angel before he was conceived in the womb.

22 And when the days of her purification according to the law of Moses were accomplished, they brought him to Jerusalem, to present him to the Lord.

23 (As it is written in the law of the Lord Every male that openeth the womb shall be called holy to the Lord ;)

36 And there was one Anna, a prophetess, the daughter of Phanuel, of the tribe of Aser : she was of a great age, and had lived with a husband seven years from her virginity.

CHAP. VII.

28 For I say unto you, Among those that are born of women, there is not a greater prophet than John the Baptist.

37 And behold, a woman in the city, which was a sinner, when she knew that *Jesus* sat at meat in the Pharisee's house, brought an alabaster box of ointment.

38 And stood at his feet behind *him* weeping, and began to wash his feet with tears, and did wipe *them* with the hairs of her head, and kissed his feet, and anointed *them* with the ointment.

39 Now, when the Pharisee which had bidden him, saw *it*, he spake within himself, saying, This man, if he were a prophet, would have known who, and what manner of woman *this is* that toucheth him : for she is a sinner.

Chap. VIII.

2 And certain women, which had been healed of evil spirits and infirmities, Mary called Magdalene, out of whom went seven devils.

Chap. XI.

27 And it came to pass, as he spake these things, a certain woman of the company lifted up her voice, and said unto him, Blessed *is* the womb that bare thee, and the paps which thou hast sucked.

28 But he said, Yea, rather blessed *are* they that hear the word of God, and keep it.

Chap. XX.

28 Master, Moses wrote unto us, If any man's brother die, having a wife, and he die without children, that his brother should take his wife, and raise up seed unto his brother.

THE GOSPEL ACCORDING TO
ST. JOHN.

Chap. III.

4 Nicodemus saith unto him, How can a man be born when he is old? can he enter the second time into his mother's womb, and be born?

Chap. IV.

17 Jesus said unto her, Thou hast well said, I have no husband:

18 For thou hast had five husbands, and he whom thou now hast, is not thy husband.

Chap. VIII.

3 And the scribes and Pharisees brought unto him a woman taken in adultery: and when they had set her in the midst,

4 They say unto him, Master, this woman **was** taken in adultery, in the very act.

7 So when they continued asking him, he lifted up himself, and said unto them, He that is without sin among you, let him first cast a stone at her.

8 And again he stooped down, and wrote on the ground.

9 And they which heard *it*, being convicted by *their own* conscience, went out one by one, beginning at the eldest, *even* unto the last: and Jesus was left alone, and the woman standing in the midst.

11 She said, No man, Lord. And Jesus said unto her, Neither do I condemn thee: go, and sin **no more.**

THE ACTS OF THE APOSTLES.

Chap. I.

18 Now this man purchased a field with the reward of iniquity; and falling headlong, he burst asunder in the midst, and all his bowels gushed out.

Chap. XII.

23 And immediately the angel of the Lord smote him, because he gave not God the glory: and he was eaten of worms, and gave up the ghost.

Chap. XIV.

8 And there sat a certain man at Lystra, impotent in his feet, being a cripple from his **mother's womb.**

THE EPISTLE OF PAUL THE APOSTLE TO THE
ROMANS.

Chap. I.

24 Wherefore God also gave them up to uncleanness, through the lusts of their own hearts, to dishonor their own bodies between themselves:

25 Who changed the truth of God into a lie,
and worshiped and served the creature.

26 For this cause God gave them up unto vile
affections. For even their women did change the
natural use into that which is against nature:

27 And likewise also the men, leaving the nat-
ral use of the women, burned in their lust one toward another; men with men working that which
is unseemly, and receiving in themselves that recompense of their error which was meet.

Chap. II.

22 Thou that sayest a man should not commit
adultery, dost thou commit adultery?

25 For circumcision verily profiteth, if thou
keep the law; but if thou be a breaker of the law,
thy circumcision is made uncircumcision.

27 And shall not uncircumcision which is by
nature, if it fulfill the law, judge thee, who by the
letter and circumcision dost transgress the law?

28 For he is not a Jew, which is one outwardly;
neither *is that* circumcision which is outward in
the flesh:

29 But he *is* a Jew which is one inwardly; and
circumcision *is that* of the heart.

Chap. III.

1 What advantage then hath the Jew? or what
profit *is there* of circumcision?

30 Seeing *it is* one God which shall justify the

circumcision by faith, and uncircumcision through faith.

Chap. IV.

9 *Cometh* this blessedness then upon the circumcision *only*, or upon the uncircumcision also? For we say that faith was reckoned to Abraham for righteousness.

10 How was it then reckoned? when he was in circumcision, or in uncircumcision? Not in circumcision, but in uncircumcision.

11 And he received the sign of circumcision, a seal of the righteousness of the faith which *he had yet* being uncircumcised: that he might be the father of all them that believe, though they be not circumcised; that righteousness might be imputed unto them also:

12 And the father of circumcision to them who are not of the circumcision only, but who also walk in the steps of that faith of our father Abraham, which *he had* being *yet* uncircumcised.

13 For the promise that he should be the heir of the world *was* not to Abraham, or to his seed, through the law, but through the righteousness of faith.

17 (As it is written, I have made thee a father of many nations.)

19 And being not weak in faith, he considered not his own body now dead, when he was about a hundred years old, neither yet the deadness of Sarah's womb.

20 He staggered not at the promise of God through unbelief.

Chap. IX.

7 Neither, because they are the seed of Abraham, *are they* all children: but, In Isaac shall thy seed be called.

8 That is, They which are the children of the flesh, these *are* not the children of God : but the children of **the** promise are counted for the seed.

9 For this *is* the word of promise, At this time will I come, and Sarah shall have a son.

10 And not only *this;* but when Rebecca also had conceived by one, *even* by our father Isaac.

11 (For *the children* being not yet born, neither having done any good or evil, that the purpose of God, according to election might stand, not of works, but of him that calleth ;)

12 It was said unto her, The elder shall serve the younger.

13 As it is written, Jacob have I loved, but Esau have I hated.

––––––

THE FIRST EPISTLE OF PAUL THE APOSTLE TO THE
CORINTHIANS.

Chap. V.

1 It is reported commonly *that there is* fornication among you, and such fornication as is not so much as named among the Gentiles, that one should have his father's wife.

Chap. VI.

13 Meats for the belly, and the belly for meats : but God shall destroy both it and them.   Now the body *is* not for fornication, but for the Lord.

15 Know ye not that your bodies are the members of Christ? shall I then take the members of Christ, and make *them* the members of a harlot? God forbid.

16 What ! know ye not that he which is joined

to a harlot is one body? for two, saith he, shall be one flesh.

18 Flee fornication. Every sin that a man doeth, is without the body; but he that committeth fornication, sinneth against his own body.

Chap. VII.

1 Now concerning the things whereof ye wrote unto me: *It is* good for a man not to touch a woman.

2 Nevertheless, *to avoid* fornication, let every man have his own wife, and let every woman have her own husband.

3 Let the husband render unto the wife due benevolence: and likewise also the wife unto the husband.

4 The wife hath not power of her own body, but the husband: and likewise also the husband hath not power of his own body, but the wife.

5 Defraud ye not one the other, except *it be* with consent for a time, that ye may give yourselves to fasting and prayer; and come together again, that Satan tempt you not for your incontinency.

6 But I speak this by permission, *and* not of commandment.

7 For I would that all men were even as I myself.

8 I say therefore to the unmarried and widows, It is good for them if they abide even as I.

9 But if they cannot contain, let them marry: for it is better to marry than to burn.

10 And unto the married I command, *yet* not I, but the Lord, Let not the wife depart from *her* husband:

11 But and if she depart, let her remain unmarried, or be reconciled to *her* husband: and let not the husband put away *his* wife.

18 Is any man called being circumcised? let him not become uncircumcised. Is any called in uncircumcision? let him not be circumcised.

19 Circumcision is nothing, and uncircumcision is nothing, but the keeping of the commandments of God.

25 Now concerning virgins, I have no commandment of the Lord: yet I give my judgment as one that hath obtained mercy of the Lord to be faithful.

26 I suppose therefore that this is good for the present distress; *I say*, that *it is* good for a man so to be.

27 Art thou bound unto a wife? seek not to be loosed. Art thou loosed from a wife, seek not a wife.

28 But and if thou marry, thou hast not sinned, and if a virgin marry, she hath not sinned. Nevertheless, such shall have trouble in the flesh: but I spare you.

33 But he that is married, careth for the things that are of the world, how he may please *his* wife.

34 There is difference *also* between a wife and a virgin. The unmarried woman careth for the things of the Lord, that she may be holy, both in body and in spirit: but she that is married, careth for the things of the world, how she may please *her* husband.

36 But if any man think that he behaveth himself uncomely toward his virgin, if she pass the flower of *her* age, and need so require, let him do what he will, he sinneth not: let them marry.

37 Nevertheless, he that standeth steadfast in his heart, having no necessity, but hath power over his own will, and hath so decreed in his heart that he will keep his virgin, doeth well.

38 So then he that giveth *her* in marriage doeth

well; but he that giveth *her* not in marriage **doeth** better.

Chap. XI.

3 But I would have you know, that the head of every man is Christ; and the head of the woman *is* the man; and the head of Christ *is* God.

4 Every man praying or prophesying, having *his* head covered, dishonoreth his head.

7 For a man indeed ought not to cover *his* head, forasmuch as he is the image and glory of God: but the woman is the glory of the man.

8 For the man is not of the woman, but the woman of the man.

9 Neither was the man created for the woman, but the woman for the man.

14 Doth not even nature itself teach you, that if a man have long hair, it is a shame unto him?

15 But if a woman have long hair it is a glory to her: for *her* hair is given her for a covering.

Chap. XII.

23 And those *members* of the body, which we think to be less honorable, upon these we bestow more abundant honor; and our uncomely *parts* have more abundant comeliness.

24 For our comely *parts* have no need: but God hath tempered the body together, having given more abundant honor to that *part* which lacked:

Chap. XIV.

34 Let your women keep silence in the churches; for it is not permitted unto them to speak; but *they are commanded* to be under obedience, as also saith the law.

35 And if they will learn anything, let them **ask** their husbands at home; for it is a shame **for women to speak in the church.**

THE EPISTLE OF PAUL THE APOSTLE TO THE
GALATIANS.

Chap. IV.

19 My little children, of whom I travail in birth again, until Christ be formed in you.

27 For it is written, Rejoice, *thou* barren that bearest not; break forth and cry, thou that travailest not: for the desolate hath many more children than she which hath a husband.

Chap. V.

17 For the flesh lusteth against the Spirit, and the Spirit against the flesh.

Chap. VI.

12 As many as desire to make a fair shew in the flesh, they constrain you to be circumcised; only lest they should suffer persecution for the cross of Christ.

13 For neither they themselves who are circumcised keep the law; but desire to have you circumcised, that they may glory in your flesh.

THE EPISTLE OF PAUL THE APOSTLE TO THE
EPHESIANS.

Chap. V.

3 But fornication, and all uncleanness, or covetousness, let it not be once named among you, as becometh saints;

4 Neither filthiness, nor foolish talking, nor jest ing, which are not convenient: but rather giving of thanks.

5 For this ye know, that no whoremonger, nor unclean person, nor covetous man, who is an idol- ater, hath any inheritance in the kingdom of Christ and of God.

22 Wives, submit yourselves unto your own husbands, as unto the Lord.

23 For the husband is the head of the wife, even as Christ is the head of the church: and he is the Savior of the body.

24 Therefore as the church is subject unto Christ, so *let* the wives *be* to their own husbands in everything.

THE EPISTLE OF PAUL THE APOSTLE TO THE
COLOSSIANS.

Chap. III.

18 Wives, submit yourselves unto your own husbands, as it is fit in the Lord.

19 Husbands, love *your* wives, and be not bitter against them.

THE FIRST EPISTLE OF PAUL THE APOSTLE TO THE
THESSALONIANS.

Chap. IV.

4 That every one of you should know how to possess his vessel in sanctification and honor;

5 Not in the lust of concupiscence, even as the Gentiles which know not God.

THE FIRST EPISTLE OF PAUL THE APOSTLE TO
TIMOTHY.

CHAP. II.

11 Let the woman learn in silence with all subjection.

12 But I suffer not a woman to teach, nor to usurp authority over the man, but to be in silence.

13 For Adam was first formed, then Eve.

14 And Adam was not deceived, but the woman being deceived was in the transgression.

15 Notwithstanding, she shall be saved in child-bearing, if they continue in faith, and charity, and holiness, with sobriety.

CHAP. V.

11 But the younger widows refuse: for when they have begun to wax wanton against Christ, they will marry.

THE EPISTLE OF PAUL THE APOSTLE TO THE
HEBREWS.

CHAP. VII.

10 For he was yet in the loins of his father, when Melchisedec met him.

CHAP. X.

4 For *it is* not possible that the blood of bulls and of goats should take away sins,

Chap. XI.

11 Through faith also Sarah herself received strength to conceive seed, and was delivered of a child when she was past age.

12 Therefore sprang there even of one, and him as good as dead, *so many* as the stars of the sky in multitude, and as the sand which is by the sea-shore innumerable.

30 By faith the walls of Jericho fell down, after they were compassed about seven days.

31 By faith the harlot Rahab perished not with them that believed not, when she had received the spies with peace.

THE GENERAL EPISTLE OF
JAMES.

Chap. II.

25 Likewise also was not Rahab the harlot justified by works, when she had received the messengers, and had sent *them* out another way?

THE FIRST EPISTLE GENERAL OF
PETER.

Chap. III.

5 For after this manner in the old time the holy women also, who trusted in God, adorned themselves, being in subjection unto their own husbands:

6 Even as Sarah obeyed Abraham, calling him lord: whose daughters ye are, as long as ye do well, and are not afraid with any amazement.

THE REVELATION
OF ST. JOHN THE DIVINE.

CHAP. XII.

1 And there appeared a great wonder in heaven; a woman clothed with the sun, and the moon under her feet, and upon her head a crown of twelve stars :

2 And she, being with child, cried, travailing in birth, and pained to be delivered.

3 And there appeared another wonder in Heaven; and behold, a great red dragon, having seven heads and ten horns, and seven crowns upon his heads.

4 And his tail drew the third part of the stars of heaven, and did cast them to the earth : and the dragon stood before the woman which was ready to be delivered, for to devour her child as soon as it was born.

5 And she brought forth a man-child, who was to rule all nations with a rod of iron : and her child was caught up unto God, and *to* his throne.

6 And the woman fled into the wilderness, where she hath a place prepared of God, that they should feed her there a thousand two hundred *and* threescore days.

13 And when the dragon saw that he was cast unto the earth, he persecuted the woman which brought forth the man-*child.*

CHAP. XIV.

1 And I looked, and lo, a Lamb stood on the mount Sion, and with him a hundred forty *and* four thousand, having his Father's name written in their foreheads.

CHAP. XVI.

13 And I saw three unclean spirits like frogs

come out of the mouth of the dragon, and **out of the** mouth of the beast, and out of the mouth of **the** false prophet.

Chap. XVII.

1 And there came one of the seven angels which had the seven vials, and talked with me, saying unto me, Come hither ; I will shew unto thee the judgment of the great whore that sitteth upon many waters ;

2 With whom the kings of the earth have committed fornication, and the inhabitants of the earth have been made drunk with the wine of her fornication.

3 So he carried me away in the spirit into the wilderness : and I saw a woman sit upon a scarlet-colored beast, full of names of blasphemy, having seven heads and ten horns.

4 And the woman was arrayed in purple and scarlet color, and decked with gold and precious stones and pearls, having a golden cup in her hand full of abominations and filthiness of her fornication :

5 And upon her forehead *was* a name written, MYSTERY, BABYLON THE GREAT, THE MOTHER OF HARLOTS AND ABOMINA-TIONS OF THE EARTH.

THE END.

CPSIA information can be obtained at www.ICGtesting.com
Printed in the USA
LVOW050810140712

290042LV00001B/427/A